ENJOY YOUR MONEY IN 12 EASY STEPS

Stepping out of your comfort zone to reach financial freedom

Ryan L. Joy

Table of Contents

Preface

Before we begin, I want to be clear on a couple of things. For one, I am not a certified financial planner, accountant, wealth management professional, or stock market guru. This book is not going to guarantee any sort of "get rich quick" scheme or offer any special "secrets" that only millionaires know.

There are dozens upon dozens of books out there that try to show you an "easy" way to get rich. In fact, I'm not even going to guarantee that you will get rich because that is an arbitrary term that is solely subjective. Each person's idea of what "rich" means is completely different, so it wouldn't make sense for me to try to explain to you how to obtain that goal.

What you will learn is a proven method that will get you to the point where you will be able to ENJOY your money – whatever that means for you.

In the following pages, you will learn how to make your money work for you – instead of constantly trying to work for money. You will learn how to get to a point in your financial life where you can do the things you've always wanted to do.

Have you always wanted to travel more? Have you found yourself saying to yourself over and over, "I can't afford that?" Do you find you spend so much time stressing about your money - that you lose sleep thinking about how you will be able to make that next payment?

Or have you simply failed to have a plan in place that is keeping you back from reaching your financial goals and dreams?

If any of those things apply, this book is for you!

Hell, I'm not even an author! But what I am is a person who decided several years ago that I was going to take control of my life, and it starts with your money.

Today, I can sit here and safely say that by going through what has evolved into a simple, 12-step process (more on that later), I have been able to make incredible, positive changes to my life.

LET ME WARN YOU. This will not be easy. It isn't until we gain control of how we spend that we will be able to control how we will be able to live.

This will take dedication, honesty, and accountability, and it will be difficult at times. But the truth is, once you get into a routine, you will find it was never really that hard.

In a world where COVID-19 had been at the forefront of our lives, impacting millions of people – leaving tens of thousands of families without work and even without food to eat – I figured there was no better time than to share our story.

Let me start by sharing our personal journey with you…

Introduction

Our story

We got engaged in 2015. Like many newly-engaged couples, the first conversation that you are excited to have is about your finances, right?

Of course not!

In fact, I would venture to guess that many of you, to this day, have not sat down and actually had a productive, concrete conversation about your financial plan.

What I hear from a lot of people is, "Well, she makes sure the bills are paid, and I don't ask questions." Or, "he sends out the checks, and I just buy things because we have the money."

It's crazy.

Some people have shown a bit more diligence by at least identifying what goes out each month. As long as you know you make enough to cover those expenses, you are good, right?

NO! Although it is a starting point.

My wife Ashley and I had two very different views on how we spent our money. To be fair, we started our life together in probably a better spot than a lot of people.

That is not a humble brag. This is being honest.

My approach to money was simple: I don't like to spend it. Because of that, I worked all the time, spent what I had to, and went out whenever I wanted. As long as I saw money in my bank account, things were okay.

I did what I wanted when I wanted, and as long as I had a little bit of money, I was living the dream. That free spirit-ness combined with a sense of responsibility, I am SURE is what got Ashley's attention!

With that said, my frugality allowed me to enter into the relationship with a shade over $7,000 to my name. I even started a small investment portfolio that had roughly $5,500 in it. Not bad!

Now my wife, on the other hand, had her shit together a little more than I did. She lived on her own (while I had two roommates), had a more stable job, was able to take care of herself, and actually had a mattress with a bedframe!

Her father had given some good advice once she started her career to always have three months of expenses in her account in case something was to go wrong. To be fair, that's pretty good advice.

The issue? She always had (and if nothing changed, always would have) three months of expenses in her bank account.

Nonetheless, she entered into matrimony with a pretty solid $12,000 to her name.

As I am writing this, we are coming up on our four-year wedding anniversary. Yes, thank you – I know – it's a wonderful accomplishment. But let's say we had never put our money to work.

It took us each about five years to accrue that much money. $20,000+! We're rich! But there's a problem with this approach; the math doesn't lead us down a lucrative road.

Sorry folks, there is a little bit of math in this book.

Let's see where we might have been now:

It took me five years to get $12,500. Say I stuck with the same habits, and my money doubled over our first five years of marriage. That means in May of next year, I will have $25,000.

That's pretty good.

Ashley, on the other hand, would have – and you may have guessed it – still $12,000. Three months of expenses to her name. Boom.

That's a grand total of $37,000.

Now, let me ask you a question. Do YOU have close to 40k in your bank account(s) right now? Probably not. The median amount of money in people's accounts in the US today is $4,500.

Not even close.

To be honest, neither do we. We have much, much more than that.

Let me get back to the story.

We were planning our wedding. What a glorious time! Did you know that the average amount spent on a wedding these days is over $25,000? Crazy, I know. For the price tag of $25,000, you get to:

- Dress up nice
- Hang out with a bunch of people you don't usually spend time with
- Party for several hours
- Eat good food, maybe
- Try not to get too drunk (too early) and ruin your day
- Dance with your mom
- Have a photoshoot
- And GET MARRIED!!!

I mean, we were never going to have another day like this in our lives! This is once in a lifetime! Or twice, or three times, or… I digress.

As I pointed out, we were going to start our lives in a pretty good spot. Maybe our parents would pitch in some money, and then we would have plenty to go around as well, so we could make this thing happen easily.

Ashley started venue shopping. For anyone who has been through it before, it is very easy to see a venue start at $10,000 or more - just to show up.

That doesn't include the dress, food, DJ, photographer, decorations, gifts, and so on.

Did I mention I was frugal?

When we got engaged, I told Ashley this was her show – but I had three rules:

1. You need to be happy about everything, no matter what
2. If someone is to break that chain of happiness, I need to be given permission to intervene (even if I have to put the moms in their place)
3. We are not taking out a loan for this damn wedding

We received $7,500 from our families towards the wedding, and she agreed to those terms (not that I would have ended it if she hadn't). I am grateful she did. In my opinion, those gifts were above and beyond, and we were very thankful to receive that much.

Looking back, I truly believe that was the moment we started to learn how to enjoy the money we had. We created a wedding budget of $5,000, including wedding bands and a honeymoon.

In the end, we worked together as a team to fashion a wonderful day – and learned that through communication and creativity, we could accomplish everything we could ever want without feeling a financial burden.

In the end, we only took $4,500 out of pocket and spent a week in Ireland for our honeymoon.

We got married in May of 2016. On the plane to Dublin, I said to Ashley, "When we get back – we're going on a budget." I wanted to be smart with our money. I didn't want to repeat the mistakes I had witnessed friends and family make. In the end, I just wanted to provide for my wife.

But also, knowing how much we STILL spent on the wedding (although much less than normal) gave me heartburn.

She replied, "Okay – but let's enjoy this first." I smiled. She was right. Those worries went away.

I didn't know it then but being smart with our wedding money allowed us to enjoy an incredible honeymoon experience. The point here is early on, undenounced to us; we were experiencing what it meant to be able to enjoy our money - because we were smart with it.

That's how we balance each other out financially.

I want to stress that it's important to find a balance that works for you. You can spend your whole life building wealth without ever getting a chance to spend some of it on things that you enjoy. At the same time, you can be irresponsible with your money – which will keep you from being able to enjoy your money at all.

The honeymoon was over too soon, and we used the next month to track all of our spending so we could set our first year's budget starting in July – and we haven't looked back since.

I mentioned that we were nowhere close to having that $37,000 as we were close to finishing up our fourth year.

In that time, we've been able to shift our net worth to $175,000, pay off all our debt, put Ashley through four years of medical school, buy a new car, travel the world, and so much more.

Best of all, when COVID hit, we had put ourselves in a position where we didn't need to stress.

Best of all, we get to ENJOY OUR MONEY and each other.

If you take nothing else from this book, at least remember this equation. Yes, more of those. But this one is good.

Remember **B.E.S.T.** Write it down, put it in your wallet or clutch, and don't forget it.

$$\text{ENJOYING YOUR MONEY} = \mathbf{B}\text{UDGET} + \mathbf{E}\text{ARNINGS} + \mathbf{S}\text{ACRIFICE} + \mathbf{T}\text{IME}^2$$

Budget – The more you stick to your budget, the better.

Earnings – The more you earn, the more you can build.

Sacrifice – The more you sacrifice the things you don't need, the more you'll enjoy what you want.

Time – This applies to two things:

- Quality time - spent with your loved ones (finding that balance)
- Physical time – the longer you are committed, the higher the rewards

For those who want to dig a little deeper, follow these 12 steps. Each one builds upon the last. It will get you to where you want to go. I thought about shaving it down to 10 steps or less, but then it wouldn't be genuine to the process we have followed.

Everyone is a little different; they come from different backgrounds and circumstances. The principles remain the same. In the end, my goal is to be able to show you how to enjoy your money – today, tomorrow, and forever.

Using our own experiences and stories as anecdotes, you will discover things that you maybe only thought were possible but never had someone show you how to get there.

I will help you along your own personal path to financial freedom.

As I mentioned before, the process is simple, but it will not always be easy. For those reasons, it is first important for you to look deep into your psyche and find out "why" you picked up this book in the first place.

The first step in the rest of your personal financial life is finding your "why."

Let's begin.

STEP ONE

FIND YOUR "WHY"

This first step could be the most important. Finding your "why" is about always being able to find your true north if you were to ever fall off course.

It's about having a constant reminder as to the reason why you are doing this in the first place.

There are entire books and courses that focus solely on this topic. But for the purpose of reaching financial freedom – where you can FINALLY get to a point where you can enjoy your money – your "why," simply put - is the reason you probably bought this book.

It's now going to be about identifying what that "why" is for you.

There is reason behind every decision we make. Take food, for example. Often, we eat food because we are hungry. Your body tells your brain that it needs fuel, and we respond by finding something to feed that need.

However, far too often we associate eating food with how we are feeling in the moment.

Have you ever had a terrible day at work, and on the way home, you stop at that fast food joint because "those french fries will make me feel better?"

Do you really need to eat those fries? Probably not.

If you dug deep into the reason why you turned to those fries, you might find there are things that dig deeper into your psyche besides the fact that you just like the taste of fries.

The same thing applies to how we spend our money.

We buy ourselves another pair of shoes because we "deserve" them. We go out and buy that cute pair of jeans because we like the way we look in them. Hell, we go out and buy that new car we can't afford because we want to be seen as successful.

Each time we spend money, there is a decision process that leads to making that purchase. Some are out of necessity ("I need to pay the rent because I need to keep a roof over my family's head"). Other purchases come from emotion ("I went to get my nails done because when I do, I feel better about myself").

Regardless of the reasons behind why you make certain purchases – if you don't know your "why," it makes it very difficult to keep yourself accountable on the road to financial success.

This "why" is known as your TRUE WHY – the cornerstone by which all your future decisions will be assessed.

Compare that to your EMOTIONAL WHY – the feeling that drives your in-the-moment decision.

Let me give you an example. You see a purse that you like at a store. You don't need that purse, but you had a good week, and it will make you feel good to be able to say that you got a nice purse today. It's basic want vs. need. As we established, you don't need the purse – but you do want it. Ask yourself why?

"I like buying purses."

Why?

"They make me feel better about myself."

Why?

"I feel that if I don't have nice things, I am not valuable."

Why?

"Because I have low self-esteem."

Why?

"Because ever since I was a child, I got picked on for my weight."

Why?

"I grew up in a household where being healthy wasn't important."

Why?

"We didn't have the money to be able to buy healthy food."

Why?

"My mother spent all of her hard-earned dollars buying new purses."

Can you see the connection?

This might be a SLIGHTLY far-fetched example, but the reality is a lot of the reasons why we buy certain things related to something much deeper that we might not be aware of at first.

Will buying that purse make you feel better in the moment? Maybe. Will it solve your inner issues of low self-esteem, weight issues, and growing up in a household that lived paycheck to paycheck?

NO!

You can't control what has happened in the past, but you can control the outcome of your future.

The emotional whys tend to blind us from making financially savvy decisions because often we only stop at the first or second why.

"I want to buy a purse."

Why?

"I like buying purses."

Why?

"They make me feel better about myself."

…and we stop right there.

This perpetuates the constant cycle of buying things that we don't really need! Never mind the fact that it does not help us out financially.

If we are able to identify our TRUE WHY, we will be able to consistently go back to it and see if our decisions are in line with our "why". Emotional whys are simply excuses we make to get things that we want.

So ask yourself. Why do you truly want to achieve financial freedom? What would you be able to enjoy if money was not an issue?

I am not saying that you cannot buy that purse. I am also not saying that money will all of a sudden shrink your waistline. The point here is that if you aren't able to justify why you buy certain things and you have not identified the most important thing(s) in your life – then you will never be able to focus on holding yourself accountable when you spend.

Another way to look at it is whether you NEED something or WANT something. This is nothing you haven't heard before, and we touched on that briefly.

Do you need that purse?

No.

Do you want that purse?

Yes.

Will it interfere with accomplishing your goals?

No.

Then buy it. If the answer is yes, or I'm not sure – then ask yourself, how will it affect my true why?

Before I continue, I want to mention that this book will not put a complete lockdown on buying things that make you happy or even having a little bit of fun. There is a built-in "just because" fund that is worked into your budget where you can buy whatever you want, no questions asked. We will touch on that later.

My true why has evolved over the last few years, but it has pretty much remained the same at its core. It goes something like this:

"I never want to have to look at my wife and tell her that we can't do something together because, financially, it will break us.

When we have children, I want to be in a place where we will be able to provide them with every opportunity they want to take advantage of.

I will never let my life go by when I look back and come to the realization that all I did was work, with nothing to show for it.

I want to be able to spend as much time as possible with the ones I love, doing the things that make us happy.

Then I want to be able to give back to all of those who helped get me there and help enrich their lives, too."

In short, I want to provide for my family, spend more time doing *things* that make me happy than work, and help others achieve the same.

And that's WHY we live on a budget. That's WHY we have made sacrifices. That's WHY I spend each day focusing on how we can accomplish just those things.

I don't buy purses, but I do buy vacations. I rarely even buy new clothes because if I were to go into a store to buy a new suit, coat, or sweater – I would stop and think about my "why."

I recommend spending some time finding what your true "why" is. Once you are able to identify it, write it down. Keep it in your wallet if you have to. Use it as your guiding light to help you make smart choices when you are faced with a decision to buy something.

I want to keep things as simple as possible for you. When making a purchase, ask yourself these three questions:

1. Do I need this, or do I want it? If you need it, don't think twice. If you want it, move to #2
2. Will it help or hurt my journey? Find any emotional why. If it will hurt or delay where you're going. Stop, don't do it. If you think it might help (or won't burden), go to #3
3. Is this in line with my "true why"? If the answer is yes – go for it. If it's not, as hard as it might be, it is for the best long term to put that thing down.

One last example using this process. Recently, I took my real estate license course. Before I did so, I asked myself those questions, and this was the thought process I had (it cost $300):

Do I need to do this? No. But I definitely want to.

Is it going to hurt what we're trying to do? No. But will it help? It could. If I wanted to make a career switch, there is some great flexibility in becoming a real estate agent, and I wouldn't have to make the one-hour commute to my sales job five days a week anymore.

Well, is it in line with my true why? Absolutely. The increased flexibility will give me more free time to be at home, and the income is directly correlated with how much I choose to put into it.

I can take a month off if I want to and still make the money I need to provide for Ashley and me. In fact, it could increase our annual income with less need to "be at work."

NO BRAINER.

So that's what I did. The $300 purchase to me was well worth it, and it has been.

Finding your true "why" isn't always easy. It's important to be completely honest with yourself and really dig into what you want to see your life looking like and the reason behind that.

Every person will have a slightly different why. Again, I urge you to give it a lot of thought and write something down; have an idea as to what your "why" is before you move on – because it will keep you focused when things get hard. At times, it will.

Saying, "I want to become a millionaire," will not cut it for most, if not all. It's too vague, and there is no emotion attached to it.

When faced with a challenge, it is much harder to say no to something if it means something to you – so I encourage you to brainstorm, take some time, and when you're done – keep that pen in your hand because we are going to start setting goals, one of my favorite things to do.

There is nothing better than setting a financial goal and crushing it.

MY TRUE WHY:

____

____

____

____

____

____

____

STEP TWO

LIST YOUR FINANCIAL GOALS

Once you have been able to identify your "why," you can now start setting some financial goals for yourself and your family. This step is not difficult, but it is important.

Be sure you WRITE YOUR GOALS DOWN.

Multiple studies have shown that those who write their goals down are more likely to achieve them. There is a certain level of accountability that you set for yourself by putting your goals to paper.

There are three things to consider when looking at your goals. I have found these to be useful in accomplishing many of ours:

1. Be specific
2. Avoid ambiguous and "unrealistic" goals
3. Set deadlines

Be Specific- It is important when you are writing down your goals to be specific in what you want to accomplish. Setting a goal for yourself to "buy a house" does not give you enough information to stay focused on the goal. Adding specifics gives you more clarity.

If your goal is to buy a house, it will be better to write down, "put away 10% of my income each month until I reach $50,000 – to allow me to put 20% down on a $250,000 home.

Avoid Ambiguity – This is also important because if you set goals that seem too far-fetched or hard to accomplish, you will never put enough time in to accomplish the goal. Similarly, it will be much harder to stick to your new-found habits if you don't see immediate progress.

A common goal people have is, "I want to be a millionaire."

Don't we all?

If your goal is simply getting to a $1 million net worth, is that realistic right now? You have $300 in your bank account and don't know how you will pay the rent next month.

What might be more realistic is to say, "I want to have $10,000 in my bank account." This still might not be easy at first, but you can reach that goal in a matter of months!

Now that the train is rolling, you might find, after a couple of years that your new habits can get you to a million sooner than you thought.

Set Deadlines – Again, this is an important facet to keep accountability. Let's use the previous example. If your goal is to have $10,000 in a bank account – if you don't set a date for yourself, we as humans inherently find easy reasons to procrastinate, and it pushes things back.

But if you say, "I will have $10,000 in my bank account by the end of this year – it will allow you to start breaking that time up into weeks and months to allow you to figure out how much you need to save to get to that goal.

I will show you how to do that later.

Let's note that dates can change – but DO NOT change your dates simply because you don't want to stick to your deadlines.

Now, we can put all these things together. I will give you a couple of examples from my life. In fact, to this day, we have a mini dry-erase board that sits on our refrigerator with our latest goal.

For me, I like numbers – and for my wife, she enjoys visuals. So, I drew one of those thermometers that you fill in as you get closer to reaching each of your goals.

While I do all the things behind the scenes, she gets a visual of how quickly we are approaching our latest goal.

GOAL: We want to become debt-free.

BETTER GOAL: We will make an additional $500 payment on our debt at the end of each month until it's all paid off.

GREAT GOAL: At the end of each month, whatever we have netted (income minus expenses), 80% of that net will go as an additional payment towards our debt. If that amount can fully pay off a loan, we will. If not, it will be applied to whatever loan has the highest interest rate until that is paid off.

We will continue to do this until each individual loan is paid in full, and we will be debt-free. We hope to do this within 36 months.

Now, I know that is a lot, but once you have gone through this book and gained a better understanding of how you can start making your money work for you, your goals will become clearer, and you will be able to write one like that.

For now, I would recommend writing down a few things that you would like to accomplish in the space provided at the end of this chapter. Don't feel like you have to go too far in-depth, but once you have completed this book, you can go back to your goals and expand on them to give you more clarity.

Here is one more example of our current goal.

GOAL: We want to buy a house.

BETTER GOAL: We want to be ready to buy a house by the time Ashley finishes school, which will be in the summer of 2021.

GREAT GOAL: Currently, we know we could afford a home no more than $325,000, based on keeping our mortgage below 25% of our monthly take-home pay.

We will not put any less than 20% down on a home, so by May of 2021, we will have $65,000 in our "down payment" account, putting X into that account each month until then.

I know that can be overwhelming. But again, once you go through all of these steps and really get a grasp on how your money moves, you will be able to set your goals like the examples above.

One more thing to note is I understand that people often have more than one goal. Especially if you are just starting out, you may have an entire list of goals that revolve around the following:

- Stop living paycheck to paycheck
- Save enough to have a cushion
- Pay off all your credit cards
- Start saving for your children's education
- Pay your home off early
- Save for retirement
- Get a new car
- And so on…

We all have many things that we want to accomplish. In fact, it is a good thing to have several goals. With that said, I want to strongly encourage you to focus on one goal at a time, at least to start.

Once you start getting the hang of things, you could potentially focus on two goals at once.

Beyond that, I couldn't tell you what to do. I know myself, and if I started to focus on more than two things at once, I would fall off course.

It is not a challenge, and I wouldn't even recommend it, but again – I would start by focusing on one goal at a time. In fact, steps five thru eight give you a good goal blueprint. Following those in order will almost guarantee future financial success.

If you want to go rogue, you can – you have free will. I just don't recommend it.

So, if you don't know where to begin, start by writing down these goals:

- Set a budget – we will put ourselves on a budget and stick to it
- Start Saving – we will start putting money away each month
- Crush our debt – we will pay off all of our debt as soon as possible
- Build a buffer – we will put ourselves in a place where we can enjoy our money

Naturally, once you go back to the goals, you will be able to expand on them.

Once you set a budget, you will be able to save.

Once you find how much you can challenge yourselves to save, you will be able to pay off your debt quickly.

Once you are debt-free, you will be able to build a buffer.

And once you have a buffer, you can focus on your larger goals.

Seems easy, right? Well, if you stick to the process, it really is!

A final thought on goals. Goals are organic, meaning you should look at your goals as a living document. Goals are also dynamic. They are ever-changing and evolving as your life continues to change and evolve. Life happens, so be mentally prepared to change your goals or focus on new goals.

Make it a habit to continually go back to the goals you have established and make changes as necessary. In my opinion, going back monthly, or even weekly, and seeing how your progress compares to your goals is a quick, simple process that helps lead towards long-lasting success.

You could be a single guy living debt-free with a good income. In three years, you are married, and in five, your first child is on the way. What happens if you marry into debt? Well, if you don't have good money habits, you could get sunk – which will lead to animosity in your new relationship.

But if you already have a budget in place and some savings – maybe even a buffer, you will be able to crush her debt quickly and start re-building that buffer.

Your goals might change in the short term, but the long-term vision and the process in which to get there will never change.

You might even find that some new "whys" come into your life, as those can change too. Regardless, you are now ready to move to the fun part – the money! Let's start with your income because everything hinges on what we bring in.

OUR FINANCIAL GOALS:

1. ____

2.____

3.____

4.____

5.____

STEP THREE

PROJECT YOUR INCOME

We have now been able to identify our "why" (or "whys"), and we have started to set some goals. We still need to accomplish a couple of things.

For the first time, we will start to look at money. It begins by looking at not only what we make but what we EXPECT to make in the future.

In general, this is an easy step. Most people get paid weekly or bi-weekly – so for anyone who is on a salary and essentially makes the same amount of money each pay cycle, this will be quick and painless.

If you are like me, with multiple jobs and multiple forms of income, coming in at different times and different times of the year – this could take a little more time – but it's still simple.

In general, I recommend setting up your income in a 12 month cycle.

The month in which you start your projections will also be the month that you begin to implement your budget.

Is there a particular month that you should start with? Not particularly. As I mentioned, our "fiscal" year runs from July-June simply because that was when we wanted to get going.

You could take that approach, but you might want to consider one of the following:

- If you run a business, being consistent with its fiscal year
- Go by calendar year to help with taxes or other reasons
- Go off of "school year". For example, teachers who choose to get paid only in months they are in school might want to start the month after school gets out and end on the last month of school.
- Seasonal jobs – if you run an ice cream stand in the Northeast, you might be closed in the winter months, so it might work around that schedule

Whatever way works for you, still go out for 12 months. I don't think it makes sense to go further because you don't necessarily know what each year brings – plus, many companies give raises on an annual basis, and so on.

If you have multiple earners (usually meaning you are married or cohabitate), it's good to project each person's income separately, even if you combine finances. If you keep your finances separate, the budget you set for yourselves will just have to dictate what money is coming out of where – but for now, we are focusing solely on income.

If you have online banking, it is easy to look back and see what money you have coming in and how often. If not, simply go off your last few pay stubs.

For those who work at a place like a restaurant where paychecks are typically smaller, you might want to track your average weekly tips for a month or so to get yourself a reasonable average expected income.

Here are two pieces of advice:

1. Be conservative in your projections. This is so you don't fall short when you start to budget; plus, it feels good to bring in more money than you anticipate.
2. Your projections should be based on TAKE HOME MONEY – not gross ("pre-taxed") income. Since the money you spend is coming out of the accounts that you have money in – it doesn't make sense to think about the money that you aren't "seeing."

Let's look at a simple, two-income family. For the sake of argument, I will use "John" as one earner and "Sarah" as the second earner. John gets paid weekly and TAKES HOME $20,000/year. Sarah gets paid bi-weekly and is projected to TAKE HOME $30,000/year.

We will use the calendar year as the starting and ending points.

We will assume that John will receive 52 paychecks and Sarah will receive 26. It is important to look at a calendar through the next year to find what months "John" will get five checks and what months "Sarah" will get three checks. These "bonus" months will, of course, happen four times a year if you get paid weekly and twice a year if you get paid bi-weekly. They are my favorite months!

EXAMPLE EXPECTED INCOME SETUP CHART

EXPECTED INCOME	January	February	March	April	May	June
JOHN	$ 1,538.46	$ 1,538.46	$ 1,923.08	$ 1,538.46	$ 1,538.46	$ 1,923.08
SARAH	$ 3,461.55	$ 2,307.69	$ 2,307.69	$ 2,307.69	$ 2,307.69	$ 2,307.69
OTHER						

EXPECTED INCOME	July	August	September	October	November	December
JOHN	$ 1,538.46	$ 1,538.46	$ 1,923.08	$ 1,538.46	$ 1,538.46	$ 1,923.08
SARAH	$ 3,461.55	$ 2,307.69	$ 2,307.69	$ 2,307.69	$ 2,307.69	$ 2,307.69
OTHER						

So, to follow this example, John received a "bonus" check in March, June, September, and December. Sarah received "bonus" checks in January and July, respectively. The projected take-home income totals $50,000.

There is a third row titled "OTHER". Perhaps John and Sarah sell Christmas trees in November and December – and that's the only time during the year that they get income in that form. You would use other anticipated income during the year in the column. This adds $3,700 for a grand total of $53,700.

Another option would be to replace the names "John" and "Sarah" with the names of the job. This is what Ashley and I do. Assume John works at Home Depot and Sarah works for the State of NH. Including the trees, it would look something like this:

EXAMPLE ADJUSTED EXPECTED INCOME SETUP CHART

EXPECTED INCOME	January	February	March	April	May	June
HOME DEPOT	$ 1,500.00	$ 1,500.00	$ 1,900.00	$ 1,500.00	$ 1,500.00	$ 1,900.00
STATE OF NH	$ 3,400.00	$ 2,200.00	$ 2,200.00	$ 2,200.00	$ 2,200.00	$ 2,200.00
TREES/OTHER						

EXPECTED INCOME	July	August	September	October	November	December
JOHN	$ 1,500.00	$ 1,500.00	$ 1,900.00	$ 1,500.00	$ 1,500.00	$ 1,900.00
STATE OF NH	$ 3,400.00	$ 2,200.00	$ 2,200.00	$ 2,200.00	$ 2,200.00	$ 2,200.00
TREES/OTHER					$ 1,200.00	$ 2,500.00

So, the total projected income for John and Sarah for the year will be $52,100.

But wait a second, Ryan – I thought you said they were going to make $53,700? Indeed I did – but remember the first piece of advice that I gave? **Be conservative with your projections**.

Knowing your anticipated income is a major step toward setting your budget.

If you notice from the first chart to the second, I set the anticipated take-home income to be slightly lower each month than what will likely happen.

This already starts to build in savings because your budget will be based on what you PROJECT to take home, not what you EXPECT today to take home, and this little nuance will make a big difference in the long run.

A general rule of thumb is you never want to spend more than you make, right? Sounds simple, but many of us still do it, and that's why you have thousands in credit card debt.

Here's why I say that now.

Let's take John and Sarah's projected income of $52,100. They will take home, on average, $4,341.67/month. With that said, if you look at a month like February, they will only take home an expected $3,700 that month – it happens a few times.

That means that when we get to setting John and Sarah's budget, it should not be more than $4,300, but here is my next piece of advice – *use your lowest monthly income as a baseline to set your budget*. So when we go into step 5 – setting a budget – remember $3,700.

This does not mean that you HAVE to be that conservative, but let's look at the numbers real quick. Say John and Sarah set a budget in their first year of $4,300.

They stick to the budget, and at the end of the year, they will spend $51,600 ($4,300 x 12). We know they will bring in AT LEAST $53,700. That's $2,100 in their pocket. Who says you can't save money on a budget?

That's a nice vacation for the two of them to celebrate.

But if we went with the recommended lower amount – a budget of $3,700 is $44,400 spent in a year ($3,700 x 12). Take-home pay is AT LEAST $53,700; the difference is…$9,300!

Remember that goal of having $10,000 in the bank account? Congratulations! You almost finished that goal in a year's time. I hope you follow.

The final thing of note. Do not project one-off forms of income, such as getting a tax return, a holiday bonus, working a camp for a week, etc. I would not incorporate any anticipated income unless you know you will get paid for at least a month.

Trust me, these become additional bonuses once we work our way through this.

In short:

- Stay conservative in your projections
- Go off take home money only
- Create a separate line for each person OR individual income stream
- Be prepared to use your WORST month as a baseline for your budget.

You're well on your way already. Using your brain at all yet? The next step is tracking your expenses – which is also fun – and very revealing.

Want to use the spreadsheet?
Email us at: njoyyourmoney@gmail.com.

STEP FOUR

TRACK YOUR EXPENSES

You know the age-old adage, "Honesty is the best policy." Well, for this step, you will have to be completely honest with yourself and don't hide anything.

If you are single, this will be easier because you don't have anyone you need to work with, but harder because you have no one to keep you accountable.

For married couples, have a conversation before you dive into this step that you will cast no judgement on what's in the past. You will commit to certain future guidelines and responsibilities in the future.

IF YOU ARE NOT COMMITTED TO SETTING A BUDGET AND STICKING TO IT (which comes up next), THEN STOP NOW – go back to your "whys," remind each other of your goals, and re-commit. If you cannot do so and still try to move forward, murky waters lay ahead.

The next time she asks you why you went golfing AGAIN, or the fourth time she gets her nails done to put you over budget – it will lead to a fight. Fighting can be avoided if you communicate, agree, and get on the same page.

I am not saying you won't have moments where things like this will come up, but the more you are open to talking about your expenses or taking the time to confirm that a purchase can be made – the better. This is not 50/50, eye-for-an-eye, or any other saying. This is a commitment to each other, or if you're single, a commitment to yourself.

I will teach you how to incorporate doing the things that you still like to do, like golfing or pedicures, but there needs to be an understanding that, especially in the beginning, and potentially for a longer period of time than you think – there will be times that you will have to say no and be willing to be told no. This is healthy and okay – as long as it doesn't become a habit.

If you use online banking, this will be much easier. If you don't use cash often (or even at all, like me), then this will be a cinch! If you are someone who uses cash, I am not going to tell you to stop doing so. I only know what had come to work for us.

If you're anything like me – when I have cash in my pocket - it is much easier for me to wastefully spend it.

There is almost something in my brain that knows when I use my card, I am taking money out of my bank account.

When I get some cash, which is not often – I have this image that it's not taking away from anything, so I can spend it on that coffee on the way home and not feel the consequences.

With that said, I am going to recommend that you go to a cashless system – or at least minimize the amount of cash you take out.

At the end of this section, I will give you some ways to deal with cash or at least some ways you can track it.

Nonetheless, the principles you will use in tracking your expenses will be the same.

If you do work cash-free, look back through your bank records and write down every dollar you have spent in the last two months. If any debit is made on your credit cards or debit cards, write these down. You spent $5.47 at Starbucks, write it down. You spent $400.16 on your car payment. Write that down, too.

Big or small, write it all down.

If you do take out cash often, or even from time to time, you can still look at your bank records, and they will tell you how much money you took out. What should you do?

Write it down.

What you are writing down is simple. All you need to do is put down the amount and where it went to. Target, McDonalds, rent, insurance, took out cash, etc.

Remember to start at the beginning of the month and write everything down from two months ago, then a separate sheet from a month ago. It will start to look like this:

$37.74   Wal-Mart

$41.97   Irving gas

$60.00   ATM withdrawal

$237.18   Car Payment

$2.18   Dunkin Donuts

…and so on.

Once you have completed your first two months, add up the total amount of money you spent each month.

Circle those numbers.

Are they surprising to you at all? There is no way you spent $6,000 last month, is there?!

Numbers don't lie.

If they are not a surprise, that means you already do a good job of at least tracking what you spend or have a good idea of what goes out each month. But if you are still living paycheck to paycheck, it's time to change your spending habits – also known in adult words as creating a BUDGET.

It is likely that you spent more than what you have recorded as well. There always seems to be that $20 here and there that seems to go missing, and you can't account for what you spent it on. Don't worry too much about that – this is a good starting point. If you want to go back more months, you can absolutely do so – but this will give you your foundation.

Once you are finished with this, it is time to start writing down, IN REAL TIME, everything you spend for the next month.

I recommend getting a small notebook. Get one for you and one for the spouse. If you want to write everything in a spreadsheet, you can do so as well – but make sure to spend time each week tracking all that you spent. I do this on Fridays.

If you do work with cash, you will have to keep your receipts. Having a notebook will let you write it down as soon as you spend money on something, in case you lose that late-night Taco Bell run receipt.

I know I have mentioned this a couple of times, but this is where you need to be honest. Don't worry about changing anything right now – just keep a record of what you are spending your money on.

What you will find during this month is you will already start to spend less, because now you are making conscious decisions on what you spend.

You will start to train yourself to think before you spend. I would not be surprised if, at the end of this month, you spend less than the previous months you wrote down.

You are already starting to make good habits for yourself.

Moving on.

You will now have, at a minimum, three months of expenses all written down. It is time to create spending categories. In business, there are all sorts of expenses (or costs). There are fixed, variable, mixed, sunk, period, opportunity, product – the list goes on and on.

Since I am not an MBA professor, we are not going to make this more complicated than it has to be. To become a money-saving guru, you will only have to focus on three costs- or rather, three expense categories:

Obligatory (fixed) Expenses: These are your monthly obligations – or what I have described in our worksheet as "bills and such." These are easy to identify because you have to pay them each month, usually.

Sometimes, they may be bi-monthly expenses or, on rare occasions, quarterly. But for the 99% of us who are just trying to make it through this world, these are our monthly bills.

They are obligatory because if you don't make the payment, in most cases, you will fall behind or get in trouble. Examples include:

- Rent/Mortgage
- Credit Card Payments
- Student Loans
- Utilities
- Taxes
- Insurance
- Car Payments

On a fresh sheet of paper, write all of these down for each month you explored. Label them "fixed," "bills," "obligations" – really whatever you want.

This is supposed to be fun as well! Grab a glass of wine.

Add up each column (May, June, and July, for example). The numbers you get for each month should be pretty much the same. Don't worry if they aren't exact. We live in New Hampshire, and our heat bill is much higher in February than it is in August. Nonetheless, we are obligated to pay the bill each and every month without fail. So, there will be a little bit of variability.

Living (variable) Expenses: These will make up almost the full remainder of all the things you spend money on.

Think of these things as what we spend on a day-to-day basis. These expenses are not necessarily "wants" or "needs" because while we need to eat food to survive, we don't "need" to go out to eat during the week.

While you don't "need" to have a car to get to work (I have met plenty of people who figure it out), you do need to put gas in your car if you're going to drive it.

In other words, these are the things we spend money on as a part of living on this Earth.

Included in this category are:

- Groceries
- Going out
- Dining
- Children
- Clothing
- Gasoline
- Recreation
- And more…

There are two primary reasons why these are considered variable expenses. The first is there is rarely if ever, going to be a time that you spend the exact same amount of money on any of these things each month – it will always be a little different.

As we get into setting a budget, we will give ourselves a maximum range of what we will allow ourselves to spend, but it's almost never the exact same amount as our car payments are.

The second reason is we have (for the most part) direct control over how much we spend on these things each month.

As we continue to make conscious decisions on spending and, ultimately, saving and building wealth – we can control what we spend on these things. Maybe buying "Corn Squares" instead of "Corn Chex" will save you money, for example.

On another sheet of paper (you might need three sheets – one for each month) – write down all your living expenses. Add them up for each month and circle those numbers. That's a lot of money, right?

The good thing is we can control this category!

Unforeseen (atypical) Expenses: This category is exactly as you may think. This accounts for expenses that you cannot plan but you can plan for.

When we start your budget in the next chapter, this will be your built-in buffer to handle things that come up from time to time which you don't see coming.

To be fair, when I have to register my car each year, I put that cost into this category of my budget because it's atypical, as it only happens once a year.

Maybe your child breaks his/her arm, and you have to bring them to the emergency room, and you're hit with a bill for $350. That was not something that (hopefully) happens often, so you would write that expense here.

You may or may not have many items on your list of expenses that fall into this category, but whether you do or you don't – write these down.

I have never had a month where we haven't had to spend something that didn't fall into our basic categories (for example, buying a birthday gift for your godson is atypical), so I am sure you will have some.

Add these up and circle those numbers.

We are going to pause for a moment and skip all the way to the ninth step – reconciling. I want to practice reconciling for a moment, as this will be a good time to do so. Once you have input everything into a spreadsheet or list, this will be easier. If not, that is okay – it might push you in that direction after you do what I'm about to ask.

In doing this correctly, you should have a number written down as the total money spent for each month (X, Y, and Z). You should also have a total for all three categories per month.

1. Total money spent in month X:

   ____

2. Total obligatory expenses in month X:

   ____

3. Total living expenses in month X:

   ____

4. Total unforeseen expenses in month X:

   ____

5. ADD LINES 2, 3, and 4 here:

   ____

If lines 1 and 5 are the same, congratulations! Repeat the same for the other two months, and it will continue to start some good habits. If those numbers are not the same, go back through your first sheet (with all your expenses written down before you categorized), and cross-reference them with your category sheets to make sure you accounted for each expense.

Again, I would recommend asking for our worksheets by emailing njoyyourmoney@gmail.com, or building your own spreadsheets. This will save you time in the long run.

In the previous step, we projected our income. As we close out this section, you will learn how to start piecing all these things together.

You may find different ways that work for you, but again, I would recommend sticking to a proven method before trying to do anything too crazy.

We are starting with the basics: why we're here, what our goals are, how much we earn, and how much we spend.

Do you remember how much income you are expecting to take home each month?

Let's tie together the last two steps to get you fully ready to start your budget. If you want to look back through those three months and write down what you ACTUALLY took home in income, you can – but we will dig much more into that soon.

For now, do this final, simple exercise:

1. My (our) projected monthly income:

    ____

2. Total number of months I tracked expenses:

    ____

3. Multiply line 1 by line 2 and write it here:

    ____

This is your expected income over a three-month time span (or the number of months you tracked)

4. Total amount spent during month X:

    ____

5. Total amount spent during month Y:

    ____

6.   Total amount spent during month Z:

____

7.   ADD together lines 4, 5, and 6 here:

____

This is the amount of money you spent over a three-month span (or the number of months you tracked)

8.   Subtract line 7 from line 3 and write it here:

____

The number on line 8 will either be positive, negative, or zero.

If the number is negative, you are most likely sinking and sinking fast. This means that you are spending more than you are making, and it is likely you are behind on payments, putting money on cards, and all other forms of financial chaos. If none of those things apply to you, consider yourself lucky to be starting on this now because you are in for a rude awakening if this continues.

If that number is positive, that's great. You are bringing in more than you spend, and you might even be starting a little nest egg for yourself.

The next few chapters will really hone in on setting a budget, cutting where you spend, and getting rid of bad habits, and you will give each dollar a task to see that money grow.

You had a positive number but didn't know where that surplus went. Go back through your expenses. Talk to each other about what other money you might be spending that you didn't account for.

In the end, YOU NEED TO KNOW WHERE ALL YOUR MONEY IS GOING AT ALL TIMES. It's the only way you will be able to get ahead.

If there is a chance that you weren't fully honest about what you spent your money on - go back to the beginning of this step and track your expenses for another month. Re-assess and you might be in a better place.

No matter where you are now if you feel you're ready to take the next step in your journey towards financial freedom, then let's get to it! I want nothing more than for you to enjoy your money like we do.

It's now time for us to set your budget. Keep your expenses nearby. They are going to help in the next step.

Take a deep breath. Pour yourself another glass of wine. Take the night off.
And come back fresh and ready to go tomorrow.

STEP FIVE

SET YOUR BUDGET

Welcome back.

I am not going to lie. This section is going to be a little intense. It is not difficult – but we are going to go over a lot of material. What I can promise you is that once you have completed this step, things will start to come to fruition.

You have already put all the work into getting ready to create a budget that works for you and your family. You have all the tools in place. Now it's time to put them down on paper.

As you have already found – a common theme in this book is to be honest with yourself and to lay everything out there. It will be important that you and your spouse agree on the terms (and the numbers) of your budget.

This is what we are going to do:

1. Define our expense categories (from the previous section)
2. Write everything down in list form
3. Leave room for fun
4. Draft an initial budget
5. Add up all line items
6. Compare your monthly take-home income
7. Make adjustments (if necessary)
8. Set the annual budget

By now, you have a good idea as to what you should spend your money on. Keep these things in the back of your mind:

1. Always leave yourself a buffer (this is consistent throughout this book)
2. Agree where you are willing to make sacrifices
3. The more you can NET (income minus expenses) each month – the faster you'll reach your goals

So, let's get into it!

Although you already have most of the tools – we will start with a fresh piece of paper. I recommend using the "budget worksheet" which can be provided as a framework.

The reason we want to start fresh is your monthly expenses will be tracked month-to-month, while your budget will be set year-to-year. Because of this, you can use the same budget sheet for the entire year.

As you get into the habit of reconciling (coming later), it will be easy for you to put down the totals you have spent each month in each category (we will also call these "line items") into your budget sheet.

That's a mouthful, I know. Stay with me.

What I can promise is after you get the hang of it, filling out your month-to-month on your annual budget sheet will take you no more than 30 minutes.

Define our Expense Categories / Write Everything Down / Leave Room for Fun

The easiest way to do this is to grab your expense sheet. Look at what you are spending money on. Simply put, you are going to start by naming the categories in which you spend your money on.

Remember that you have obligatory, living, and unforeseen expenses that make up the entirety of what you spend.

Start with your obligatory expenses (rent/mortgage, utilities, car payments, etc.), and work your way down.

For each monthly obligatory expense that you have, put them in "column A" or on the left side of your piece of paper. Give each item a name. Each of these is a subcategory from your tracked expenses.

For reference, here is mine:

- Rent
- Insurance
- World Vision (charity donation we make each month)
- Cable/Internet
- Electricity
- Netflix
- Cell Phones
- Water/Sewage
- Heat

- Planet Fitness

If you have car payments, I would list each car payment separately. If you have student loans or credit card payments you make each month, again – list them all separately.

Eventually, you will start paying a lot of these things off, and then they will disappear. In our first year of marriage, this list was MUCH longer. But again, give each item a name that you will remember. Instead of electricity, for example, you might want to put down "Unitil" or something like that.

Once you have those all written down, it is time to look at your living expenses, which will vary from family to family – but again – give them each a name.

You will need to decide what subcategories you are going to identify – as well as what you are going to name them. So draw a horizontal line across the sheet of paper, and continue writing down the left side of your paper.

Ours looks like this:

- Planet Fitness

- Groceries
- Dining
- Gas
- JB/Unforeseen

You will see that the last line is to account for unforeseen expenses. These do come up, and it's important to make them a part of your budget.

It's that easy!

The first two parts are done – so it's time to leave a little room for fun.

You will see that we have listed the letters "JB" in the same category as unforeseen expenses. That is our budgeting "fun" money; it stands for "just because."

Here are a couple of examples of what will fall into this category:

Why did we decide to go out with friends for drinks on a Friday night?

"Just because."

Why did I end up going golfing?

"Just because."

This is not something that you HAVE to do – and in fact, it might be easier for you as you get started to have "FUN $$$" as a separate line item in your budget instead. This is fine.

What I can tell you, though, is without having a set amount of fun money incorporated into your budget – you will either lose your mind, lose track of spending, or lose your spouse.

There is no need to crack completely down and say that you can no longer enjoy your life!

You see, what will end up happening is you will end up feeling guilty when you go out to buy that new pair of shoes for the gym, EVERY TIME.

I would be lying if I said I didn't want you to feel guilty from time to time – but that is too strong of a word. What I want for you is to be CONSCIOUS of what you are spending – to put you in a position when you are doing/buying something "just because" or "for fun" that you take that split second to ask yourself, "Is this still in our budget?", or "do I really need this right now?" So again, it is up to you – but for the sake of saving a lot of fights, both internally and relationally – put it in your budget.

Take my word for it.

Congratulations! You have the framework for your budget set. I want to point out that every month from now on when you spend money on something, you will put that amount into one of these subcategories. That is where our receipt tracking worksheet is there to help you do.

Everything written down on your current list will also be written on that sheet, so there is the perfect consistency.

Draft an Initial Budget / Add up all Line Items

You will now give values to each of your subcategories. On the same sheet of paper, all the way to the right, write down the word "budgeted" at the top.

Some you will not have control over (such as the mortgage), while others you will have to discuss and agree on what you are willing to spend.

The easiest way to work through each line item is by following the chart below:

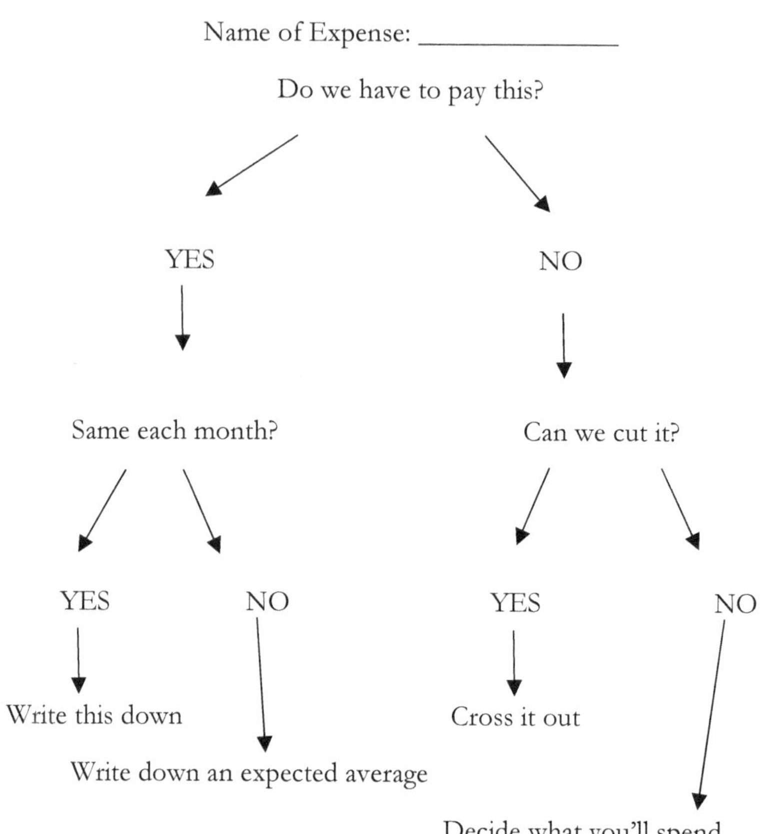

There will really only be four outcomes as you go through each line item.

I will give you some examples.

- Name of expense: Rent. Do we have to pay for this? Yes. Is it the same amount each month? Yes. Say the amount is $1500/mo. – that would be what you write down.
- Name of expense: Heat. Do we have to pay for this? Yes. Is it the same amount each month? No, it varies from month to month. In that case, you can do one of two things:
   o Write down what you think will be the average each month
   o Write down for budgeting purposes what your WORST (most expensive month) will be. This will give you another buffer for most months when it ends up being less.

- Name of expense: Planet Fitness. Do we have to pay this? No. Are we willing to cut it? Yes, we don't go to the gym ever. Simple. Stop paying for it.
- Name of expense: Donation to charity. Do we have to pay for this? No. Are we willing to cut it out of the budget? No. Decide what you're willing to budget. We give $35 to World Vision each month.

Not all decisions are going to be that easy. For example, do you REALLY need cable? No. But I am sure that is a luxury that you like to have, so set a budget on what you are willing to spend on cable each month. Maybe it means you have to get rid of all the movie channels.

The more you cut, the quicker you will get to financial freedom – so have these open conversations.

As for things like groceries, you can still cut there as well. It just means you need to shop a little smarter. I would suggest looking at what you have spent on average on groceries in the last three months and cutting it by 10%.

Obviously, it's something you have to pay for, and you can't cut it out of the budget – so agree on a number and stick to it.

If you get a month or two into your annual budget and you find that there is no way in hell you can stick to the number you set for yourself, simply adjust it – or let it be, take the hit, and adjust it again next year.

With all the buffers you have in place, even if you go over on a category or two, the ultimate goal is to be able to net (take-home income minus expenses) in the positive each month – so you can start putting money towards your goals.

Continue down line by line until you have a number written down for each line item. While you are at it, add everything up when you are done.

This is what ours looks like:

- Rent $1500
- Insurance $150
- World Vision $35
- Cable/Internet $125
- Electricity $90
- Netflix $15
- Cell Phones $100
- Water/Sewage $40
- Heat $110

| - | Planet Fitness | $25 |

-	Groceries	$400
-	Dining	$350
-	Gas	$300
-	JB/Unforeseen	$400

MONTHLY TOTAL   **$3,640.00**

This will be the MAXIMUM AMOUNT that you will spend each month over the next year.

Now, you have set the first draft of your budget. You are very close to having it done, but before we can check this box, we want to cross-reference this amount and see how it relates to income, among other things. We will make final adjustments, if needed, right at the very end.

Take a moment and see how this compares to the last three months you tracked. You may have already started to make some cuts to costs before you even put this into motion. That is great news. If this is more than what you are spending – that is okay for the moment.

This is a rough draft.

Compare Your Monthly Take-Home Income / Make Adjustments

You are close to having your budget completed. In fact, did you know that a budget is simply *an estimate of income and expenditure for a set period of time?* That's all we are doing here, folks.

We have a baseline for our expenses and projected income, and we are doing this year to year.

Speaking of income, you have already tracked this over the last couple of months. You have also projected your expected income over the rest of the year. What we want to do now is some simple math.

$$(\text{Projected monthly income} - \text{Projected monthly budget}$$
$$= \text{Net Income} / \text{Net Loss})$$

Projected Monthly Income: For the purpose of setting your budget, I would recommend using the month that you will earn the least amount of money. Find a "normal" month with no bonuses (additional paychecks as discussed in Step 3). Again, we are setting buffers everywhere.

You can use average monthly take-home income, but it could set you up for a loss for some months. We don't want that.

Projected Monthly Budget: This is the sum of all your line items ($3,640 in the example above).

Now, this is VERY IMPORTANT. If you have a NEGATIVE number – you will need to go back to the drawing board. See where you can make more cuts.

Take a deep breath.

Remember how I said that this wasn't always going to be easy? Remember your why.

You will get through this.

Look at your life now and remind yourself of the goals you have and where you want to be financially.

You can do this.

Do you know what the worst day of the year is for a coach?

Cut day.

Do you know what the best day of the year is?

The day after making cuts.

This is because the coach has his/her new team, and the excitement and anticipation that grows with where the season could go makes them forget about the difficult decisions they had to make the day before.

Today might be a cut day for you. Make those hard choices now. They will pay off. I promise.

If you simply cannot do anything else to cut your budget – you might need to find another means of income.

That is what I did to help put Ashley through school. Waiting tables to get us through. I only had to do that for a little under two years.

The hope is that the number is positive. This does not necessarily mean that you don't have to still make cuts. This simply means you are expecting to take home enough money to cover the expenses you are budgeting for yourself.

Remember John and Sarah? In Step 3, we used an example of how you can get to your financial goals much quicker by spending less now.

Quick Tangent.

I am happy that you have your expenses covered – but why are you really here? What do you want to accomplish? What can you sacrifice now to get that number lower? A few hundred bucks a month can make a huge difference.

Maybe you have hundreds of dollars in car payments, but you are barely scraping by. My advice. Get rid of them. Cars are one of the NUMBER ONE factors that keep people from reaching their financial goals. If you cannot pay for a car outright, get something else.

If you have no other option, find a payment that you can pay off early and still leaves room in the budget.

I digress… again.

We will do a little more simple math really quickly. Take your Net Income number and multiply that by 12. That is how much you should have to work with over the next year.

The next steps will tell you what you should be doing with that money to get you to the point where you can enjoy it sooner. Play with it. If I make a cut here, my bottom line is X. If I drop this a few dollars here, we can gain this much more over the year.

Many sources out there say you should save at least 20% of your income. Because we are smarter than the average bear, and we have set up buffers everywhere – using this recommendation, we would be saving 20% of our take-home pay, not 20% gross.

So, if you expect to take home $5,000/month, your budget should be no higher than $4,000 – if you want to go that route.

Ashley and I have had about a 45-55% save rate. There are many stories out there of people who go up to 80%. To us, that was too intense. For you, it's about starting somewhere.

Set the Annual Budget

Once you have made a few adjustments to your initial budget and have gotten to a number you can agree on, you are now ready to set your final annual budget.

This is the first year of the rest of your life!

I will continue to encourage you to get used to working with spreadsheets – they will make your life so much easier, as they are more efficient, and you are less likely to lose things. Never mind if you make a mistake!

The worksheets can all be provided to you. If you wish to continue on paper, then get a fresh sheet and make sure it's in landscape (the "long way") so you have a little more room to work with.

Follow These Steps:

- On the left, write down all of your expenses
- On the far right, fill out the amounts you decided for your final budget
- Across the top, write out each month in order, starting with the month you are going to begin
- In the bottom right corner, write down your total monthly budget
- Just below that, write down your annual budget. This is your monthly budget multiplied by 12.

Once you've gone through the full year, you will want to make sure that your total amount spent is below that number.

One last thing…

I want to provide one more piece of insight when it comes to your budget. Do not spend more on a line item simply because you know you are going to spend less on another. Look at each sub-category in your budget as its own "micro-budget."

If you know you will spend $50 less on groceries one month, don't go out to eat one more time just because you know you will still be under the big number at the end of the month. Again, you have been inundated with buffers.

You will have a lot more success (and see more money) if you don't.

Just don't.

If you pay off a loan within the year, for example – you now don't have $300 more to spend each month. That will go in as a $0 in your spreadsheet for each subsequent month.

Guess what?! That means you have $300 more each month to go to savings, pay off your other debts, and so much more! These are all the things we will go through as we continue.

Take a break. You deserve it.

STEP SIX

START SAVING

You now have your budget set. You should be proud of yourself for getting this far. You now have a built-in system to start saving money.

There are a lot of resources out there that talk about saving – and there are different amounts people say you should strive to save.

We all know our long-term financial goals – and this is a step that will give you more confidence to prove to yourself that you can do this.

You are going to want to start by choosing a set amount of money that you would like to save.

You don't want it to be too small – like $100 – because that will be too easy, and all good things take a little bit of work. There should be a little bit of pain or effort. What do workout coaches always say? "No pain, no gain." Well, it's a little like that.

Likewise, it wouldn't be prudent to set your initial savings goal too high. For example, while you might like to get to $10,000 saved someday (or more) – that could take a good amount of time at first.

Before I give you my recommendation, I want to give you a little bit of background on what this money's purpose really is. In reality, it is going to accomplish a couple of things:

- This will prove to you that you can, in fact, save money, which will turn into building wealth long-term
- It will give you a "mini goal" to set for yourself, and it will give you a small taste of victory
- It will give you a cushion in case something catastrophic were to happen, and you will be ready for it – without taking away from your budget.

This is setting up what many people call an "emergency fund" – money that you have put away in case of an emergency.

Now, I want to emphasize that point. This is not money you are saving for a vacation, or for a new car, or even to get that new piece of patio furniture.

This is money you are saving only in case of an emergency. In other words, once you have that money saved up, we are going to have you move that into a new account and (hopefully) NEVER TOUCH IT. The new account will come when we go over reconciling.

In the simplest of terms, once you accomplish your initial savings goal, that money DOES NOT EXIST. This is why I recommend putting it into a different account, but you don't have to do that right away.

This leads to my recommendation – and I have two.

Choose the path you are most comfortable with. There is no wrong answer. The route you choose could also be based on where you are currently.

Recommendation #1: Save $1,000

If this seems like a lot of money to you right now, this might be the best option to choose. I can assure you can do this. $1,000 is closer than you might think.

If you want a little peace of mind, simply subtract your monthly budget from your expected monthly take-home income. What number did you come up with? Well, divide one thousand by that number. That's how many months it will take for you to accomplish this goal.

If you have thousands and thousands in debt, this could be the best option for you.

I would also recommend this option if you have been living paycheck to paycheck or simply cannot afford to take $1,000 right now and put it away. Or, of course, if you don't have that much in your bank account at the present moment – this might be the best option for you. With that said, if you have at least $1,000 in your account, or you could easily put $1,000 away and not think about it – I would go with my second recommendation.

Recommendation #2: Save one month's budget

I like to recommend this option simply because this is the option we went with. I also like this option because it will get you a jump start on step 8 – build your buffer.

You already know what your monthly budget is, so your goal will be to save that amount of money, and then DON'T TOUCH IT – if I haven't said that already.

For example, if your budget is $4,500/month, that will be the amount that you want to save. Again, if you want to see how long that will probably take you, subtract your monthly budget from your monthly expected take-home income. Then divide $4,500 by that number.

If it is going to take you more than six months to save this much money, it would be smart to go with option number one. Especially if you have a lot of debt weighing over your head. It is quite possible the amount of interest you are paying on your debt will be more than what you are saving, which means you are LOSING MONEY.

IMPORTANT NOTE: If you are behind on payments, make sure to get yourself current on all your bills before you proceed with this step. If you are behind on your bills, the extra money you have each month needs to go to paying lenders back ASAP.

Once you get current, you can then refocus that extra money on savings.

However, if you are up to date on all your bills, even if you do have a lot of debt – it is important for you to show yourself that you can pay all your bills, chisel away at your debt, and put money away. You can use this chart to help make a decision (assuming your bills are current):

AMOUNT OF DEBT

	LOW DEBT	**HIGH DEBT**
$ IN ACCOUNT **COMFORTABLE**	**SAVE ONE MONTH'S BUDGET**	**CHOOSE AN OPTION ($1000 PREFERRED)**
NOT COMFORTBLE	**CHOOSE AN OPTION**	**SAVE $1000**

You can see that even if you do have a lot of debt – if you have a comfortable amount of money in your bank account right now – the choice is up to you.

Ashley and I started in this box. We had a lot of debt, but I personally liked the idea of being able to put money away while I was paying off debt.

We kind of did steps six through eight simultaneously. I will explain that more in the next couple of chapters.

Some people will tell you this is insane – you need to get rid of what you owe as soon as you can. I am not discrediting that argument. I am simply saying that for us, this is what worked.

Your journey is your own.

If you want to get rid of your debt as soon as you can, save $1,000 and start crushing it right away. If you want to have a little more money built up before throwing all of it towards your debt - that can be done too. "To each their own" is the cliché, but you would not be wrong in getting an initial bit of savings and then hitting your debt hard.

Finally, if you are fortunate enough to already have $1,000 (or even one month's budget), and it's comfortable for you to move that money and forget about it – great! You're ready to move on to the next step.

Here's what you should do now:

1. Open another bank account (second checking or savings is fine)
2. Transfer the money from your primary checking into that account
3. DON'T TOUCH IT – FORGET ABOUT IT

You don't have to overcomplicate things. It's easy to go online and open another account. Some banks have a minimum deposit needed for you to open an account. But you have at least $1,000 - that should be more than enough to open the account.

Should they offer a debit card with the account – I would take it. If you don't have the perseverance yet (and only you know yourself) to keep from tapping into your savings, maybe you don't want to.

Another thing you can do is keep that debit card in a drawer somewhere you'll remember – away from your wallet – to use for an emergency only.

If you do end up withdrawing from this account when it drops below the amount you set for yourself, you will need to go back to this step before re-engaging step seven.

Once you've gotten back to your set amount ($1,000, for example) – you can proceed again.

Which leads to one of my favorite parts of this entire process – CRUSHING DEBT. Nothing feels better than paying off that last payment.

To finish out this step, here is your homework:

1. Decide how much money you are going to save
2. Figure out how long it will take (in months) to reach that goal

You may have figured out by now this will take some time. While it only took you fifteen minutes to read this chapter, it might take you a few months to be ready for the next step.

That is okay.

This book is meant to be something you can continue to come back to. It is still good to be prepared for what to do next.

Ready to start crushing it? Me too. Let's go.

STEP SEVEN

CRUSH YOUR DEBT

Now that you have saved up a bit of money, you have proven to yourself that you can not only control your spending, but also consciously determine where your money is going to go.

As an added bonus – you have a little bit of cash! Nice job – you are on the right track. Whether you decided to save $1,000, one month of expenses, or another amount you determined – remember, that money now does not exist – unless you end up in a dire situation where you have to tap into it.

In the event that occurs – replenish your account and come right back here to crushing debt.

Let's face it. Debt is not fun. If you are like me, I do not enjoy owing anyone any amount of money, ever. To be frank, debt is often an option that is forced upon us – and it's not always a bad thing, but it is paramount that we don't take on debt that we cannot pay off in an expedited amount of time.

If we look at two of the largest purchases most people will ever make – their homes and their cars – even the structure of the payments is set up for us to fail.

In the case of a house, the average amount of time a family stays in their first home is 11-12 years. It only goes up to 14-15 years for second homes.

What is the most popular mortgage? 30 years!

Often, we get these mortgages because the payments are more affordable.

Have you ever looked at how much money you will end up paying if you actually made the payments over the course of 30 years? It's mind-blowing.

Let me do that for you.

Let's say the average home price in the United States is a shade over $225,000. Let's assume, for lack of argument, that you borrowed the full $225,000. On a 30-year fixed mortgage at 3.5% interest, by the time you pay off the house, you will have paid $363,726. That's $138,726 in interest alone.

If you take that same amount of money and divide it by 30 years, you will have $4,624.20/year. Say you chose to invest that amount each year. Starting at $0 – investing that much annually over the next 30 years will earn you $365,580 (assuming a modest 6% annual return).

In other words, the interest alone would have paid the home off completely at the end of 30 years, and you still have the $225,000 in your pocket. This is not an investment book – but that is absolutely insane! But you can afford the $3,000/month mortgage, and you need that home, right?

Even with cars. The average amount of time a person keeps a car is about 5-6 years. The average price of a car is a little over $35,000 – with average interest rates at 6%. Some of the most popular loan terms are at 60 months.

If you even kept that car – by the time you are done making payments, you will have spent $40,598. Not to mention, you have monthly car payments of more than $600. That's insane.

If you invested $600/month into an account at a modest 6% annual return, at the end of five years, you will have $40,587. Hell, you could drive around a beater for a few years – save the $600 payment in a savings account and pay for that car IN CASH.

It's not a coincidence that the numbers are almost exactly the same: forwards and back. But those who take on debt go backward. Those who don't have debt continue to move forward.

In the end, when you have debt, you pay interest. When you pay interest, you lose money. When you lose money, you are preventing yourself from being able to accumulate wealth and get to financial freedom.

When you are paying someone else, you are not paying yourself. If you're not paying yourself, then why the hell are you working your ass off to come out with nothing? This is a question that many people ask, but they don't know how to get out of the debt spiral.

That is why I want to help you.

There are many different sources out there that give you ways to tackle your debt. I will not tell you my methods are better than the next – but I will tell you that the way we do things works. So, let me draw it out for you.

In short, if we can avoid debt at all costs – do it. But it is likely a big reason why you chose to pick up this book in the first place because, like me many years ago, you have collectors calling you several times a day, and you can't afford to make the payments they are asking for, and you are so stressed out that you can't sleep at night.

It weighs on you heavily.

Let me be clear: I did not say avoid YOUR debt. I'm saying don't take on any more debt. If you have thousands that you owe, it is time for you to stop putting things on your credit cards, stopping taking out new loans, stopping – well – just stopping.

You got yourself into this.

It's time to own it, take it head-on, and crush it now.

Today.

Not tomorrow.

Today.

I don't use a lot of quotes in my writing, but there are a couple of quotes that I love when it comes to debt that I want to share – because I believe they concisely exude the prominent points I want to make in this chapter.

QUOTE #1:

"We all think we're going to get out of debt."

– Louie Anderson

While this is not very profound – I do think the comedian makes a very good point here.

The story is he continues to speak about how his family was on welfare – but the point I want to make here is that everyone *thinks* that we are going to get out of debt.

Once upon a time, I *thought* I was going to be a professional baseball player. Why didn't I make it? Well, there might be a lack of super-human athleticism – but I didn't put in enough effort either.

When you *think* you are going to do something, the thought means nothing if you don't put it into passionate action. You need to become OBSESSED with paying off your debt.

You already have all the tools to do it – so it's time to start chipping away.

QUOTE #2:

"The man who never has enough money - enough to pay his debts - has too much of something else."

– James Lendall Basford

This re-iterates some things that you have already learned when you went through your budget. You might have too many material things. Perhaps you simply spend too much on bottled water.

Whatever your vices, if you aren't able to pay off your debts, then you need to look at what you do have and figure out what you need to get rid of.

I want to promise you this – while it will be hard in the short term – in the long term, you will be able to buy Fiji water only again. The difference? This time, it will be because you can afford it.

The best thing is that you will feel good about it, which leads me to the last quote.

QUOTE #3:

"What can be added to the happiness of a man who is in health, out of debt, and has a clear conscience?"

– Adam Smith

There isn't a whole lot more to say than what has already been said by Mr. Smith.

Can you imagine being able to make a purchase without having to think about what's being taken away? How great is it a world when you want to go on that vacation or go big on your child's next birthday and not be fearful of whether it will hurt your financial obligations?

It's an amazing feeling – and you will get there too.

The process is simple. The focus and determination that you need is the hard part. How intense you want to get with it is totally up to you.

Do you remember the net income equation we looked at in the budgeting chapter? You don't? THIS IS SERIOUS.

No, that is okay – I will provide it for you again:

(Projected monthly income – Projected monthly budget
= Net Income / Net Loss)

However, you already know your monthly income, and you have already set your budget – so we will make one change. Instead of "projected", we will use the word "actual":

(Actual monthly income – Actual monthly budget = Net Income / Net Loss)

You've already set things up where you know you can put money away, too – so let's simplify it more:

(Monthly income – Actual amount spent = Net Income)

I got rid of "net loss" because we are not going to have to worry about that anymore. Will it happen sometimes on a month-to-month basis? It could. So we pivot, adjust, make more cuts, and get in the black again.

What you spend each month will also vary, so you will use what you actually spent each month to find your number.

But the "secret" to crushing your debt is simply remembering the above equation – because I know you won't forget it this time. What you have left over each month goes towards your debt. I'll give you a practical example. Let's bring back John and Sarah.

QUESTION: John and Sarah just finished their budget and decided to start at the New Year. They agreed to cap their monthly spending at $4,000. After looking at their take-home income, John realized that he brings home $400/week from Home Depot, while Sarah brings home $1,750, paid bi-weekly.

They had a great holiday season, bringing home $2,000 in Christmas tree sales in December. Because of all the gifts they bought for the family, they ended up spending over budget, with an actual amount spent of $4,300. How much money will they have available to go towards debt on December 31st (assume four weeks in December)?

ANSWER: We break it down using the equation above.

First, we need to find the take-home income for John and Sarah during the month of December. Remember that John gets paid weekly, and Sarah gets paid every other week.

<u>Income</u>

John: $400 x 4 weeks = $1,600

Sarah: $1,750 x 2 weeks = $3,500

Christmas tree Sales = $2,000

TOTAL INCOME = $7,100

<u>Spending</u>

Actual Monthly Budget = $4,000

Actual Amount Spent = $4,300

$$\text{Monthly Income (\$7,100)} - \text{Actual Amount Spent}$$
$$(\$4,300) = \textbf{\$2,800 Net Profit (Income)}$$

So John and Sarah have $2,800 dollars to work with this month.

Remember that we use what was actually spent this month to come up with our final dollar amount. Of course, when you are doing this at home, the numbers will almost never be whole dollar amounts, but this makes it easy to follow.

This was a good month!

If you had $2,800 – what would you do with it? If you said anything other than put it towards debt, come back to me here. Remember, we are crushing debt, have some money to play with, and we want to get rid of it as soon as possible.

Debt is the priority.

When deciding what to do with your money, you have a couple of options. As I mentioned, how intense you go is totally up to you.

I will offer three recommendations for you to choose from. You can also change options at any time if you choose.

Option #1: 100% ALL IN

This first option is for those who really want to go extreme with crushing their debt. The concept is very simple. Whatever you have left over at the end of each month, 100% of that will go as an additional payment towards your debt. Additionally, because you are still making your monthly obligatory payments, they are built into your budget.

In the case of John and Sarah, they would make a $2,800 payment once they close out December towards their debt.

Option #2: 80/10/10 Rule

This was the path Ashley and I took.

As I mentioned, we preferred the thought of being able to crush our debt while building our buffer at the same time. I also wanted to start investing more intensely because I didn't start until I was maybe 30 years old.

This is a little more complicated, and to be up front, because I was working multiple jobs, we had a little more wiggle room to move money around.

This might not end up being your preference – but again, this method worked very well for us. I think in the end, I didn't like the idea that once I had no debt, I would also not have much money – so I started building funds and paying back loans simultaneously.

Again, the concept is simple. We took 80% of what we profited (netted) each month and made an additional payment towards debt.

10% then went into our savings.

The final 10% went into the investment account that I started.

In the case of John and Sarah, they would have put $1,960 towards their debt, $280 into savings, and $280 into investments.

Option #3: The Coin Flip (50/50)

I am throwing this in as an option because I know that there will be some readers who are still a little hesitant to make very large payments towards their debt.

Believe me, the first time I wrote a check for more than $4,000 and gave it all to the creditors, a chill went down my spine, too. I hate seeing money go out – and checks of that size are a doozy. With that said, remember your "why".

Remember why you are doing this.

Think about how it's going to feel when you get that last intrusive phone call or receive the title to your car for the first time in your life.

I call this a coin flip because it is going to take longer for you to pay off all your debt – and that can get frustrating. But it also could give you more money to work with. Some other advisors out there may steer you away from an option like this, but if you are comfortable with it taking longer to become debt-free – I mean fully comfortable – go for it.

I also want to make this point. If you are putting 50% as an additional debt payment each month, you have to have specific purposes for where that other money is going to go. If you desperately need a new car, then the other 50% could go to that. If your child needs braces, maybe you will use the money for that purpose.

DO NOT just let that money fall by the wayside – you will spend it. So again, give a specific purpose for that money.

You could also split the other 50% into sub-categories, such as 20% to a new car you want to pay cash for, 20% into savings, and 10% into investing – for example. But again, I cannot stress this enough – you want to pay your debt off ASAP. This will take longer and get too complicated. You are just starting off.

Baby steps. Has anyone ever heard that somewhere before?

If John and Sarah went this route, they would make an additional payment towards debt of $1,400. The other half would go towards their other current financial goal.

ONE THING OF NOTE: When you pay things off ahead of time, monthly payments may go away. In other words, I remember having a student loan that, once I started making big payments on it, the system said I didn't owe my next monthly payment until several months down the road because I paid ahead of schedule.

DON'T FALL FOR THIS.

Make sure that you choose the option to continue to make your monthly payments – this is just an overpayment. Don't worry – you have it in your budget already.

Let's do a little more math – because I know that you love it so much.

The average amount of debt in the United States is $137,000. This most likely includes what people owe on their homes. But that is still debt. John and Sarah are an average family (don't tell them that), so let's see how long it would take them to pay off their debt using the three methods. We will assume every month is the same for them:

- 100% all in: $137,000/$2,800 = 49 months to pay this off, or 4 years, 1 month

- 80/10/10 rule: $137,000/$1,960 = 70 months to pay this off, or 5 years, 10 months
- 50/50 coin flip: $137,000/$1,400 = 98 months to pay this off, or 8 years, 2 months

Of course, this will be a little less than those numbers because you are still making monthly payments, but we won't make it too complicated.

Looking at these options, you can see why the 50/50 method might be a little discouraging. If you can see the light in 4-5 years- versus closer to ten - it might keep you more motivated.

You can always play with these numbers, too.

If you have multiple loans, which is pretty much everyone, I would also like to make some recommendations on what loans you should pay off first.

What Debts Should I Pay Off First?

I have said this a few times, but there are a lot of resources out there that tell you how you should pay off your debt. You may have heard of the "snowball" strategy or the "avalanche" debt method. Why they all involve the winter months, I am not sure – but our strategy took some aspects of both. Again, the approach you choose must work for you, but I will share these popular options – and then what we did instead.

Snowball – This strategy involves essentially paying off your lowest loan amounts first. The theory behind this is that once you have paid off a loan, you now have that additional money available that can allow you to make larger debt payments to your next lowest loan, where it will start to "snowball" until you have fewer loans that you need to pay off with more and more money you can throw at it until you pay them all off.

Avalanche – This strategy has you take all of your loans and arrange them by putting them in descending order by interest rate, regardless of how large the loan balance is. In other words, the loan that has the highest interest rate you should pay off first and then work your way down from there. The theory behind this is you are saving money over time because you aren't losing money in interest rates.

My method – I don't have a creative name for the method that I use – but if you have any good ideas, feel free to send them my way! I was thinking about calling it the "ripple effect", but it didn't feel quite right.

Either way, we took a similar approach to the previous strategies, taking aspects from both.

We listed all of the accounts in which we owed money. Student loans, credit cards, car payments, etc. We arranged the accounts by interest, high to low, much like the avalanche method however, if there was a month where what we would put in as an additional payment would PAY OFF one of the accounts – we would pay that off, which is sort of like the snowball.

Additional monthly payments were applied to whichever had the most owed, with the highest interest rate. In my eyes, that was the account that accrued the most interest in that month, so I want to pay that down.

Here is a visual to make it easier:

NAME OF LOAN		AMOUNT OWED	INTEREST RATE
A.	CAR	$14,000	5.9%
B.	NAVIENT	$12,000	6.2%
C.	GOVT LOAN	$13,000	6.2%
D.	CREDIT CARD	$2,500	10.4%

If you used the snowball method, you would pay off your loans in the following order: D, B, C, A.

If you used the avalanche method, you would pay off your loans in the following order: D, B, C, A,

If you used the ripple method, you would pay off your loans in the following order: D, B and C (whichever has the highest amount left in that month), then A.

So if you had $4,000 that you could put in this month, you would pay off the $2,500 CREDIT CARD – which will leave you with $1,500.

You would then apply that $1,500 to NAVIENT (B), leaving it at $10,500.

I realize that if you tried to figure out month after month what interest is accruing for each account, you can. If you want to drive yourself crazy, you can try to figure it out and always pay that one down. I think that is a lot of wasted time.

Keep it simple.

This cycle will continue month after month until all your debt is paid off. Our debt worksheet can be provided if you want to see how to set everything up in Excel. Simply email us at njoyyourmoney@gmail.com. It will even give you an idea of how long it will take to pay off each loan and all your debt overall.

I want to stress that paying down your debt needs to be at the absolute forefront of your mind during this time. Trust me, it will be worth it.

Even if it is a couple of hundred bucks each month, it will accelerate the amount of time that it will take for you to be debt-free.

It took us 45 months, so yes – you will be on this step for potentially a long time. The thing is, you will start realizing that when you actually spend less than you budget each month, it opens up more for you to apply to your debt at the end of the month.

You'll be able to SEE the benefits of frugality.

Work out the numbers, set a goal for yourself, and start crushing your debt!

Debt Forgiveness

One last thing I want to touch on is debt forgiveness. There are a lot of companies out there that say they will help you get out of debt for pennies on the dollar.

Be very careful with these because they can have some serious long-term negative effects on your credit and overall livelihood.

Essentially, companies like these work with the lenders to offer to pay off your loans on your behalf. When people don't pay their loans back, you can go into delinquency, and sometimes even worse – like garnishing your wages, etc.

Sometimes, the lenders would rather get SOMETHING from you than nothing, so they will negotiate with you to pay a lower amount.

DON'T DO IT.

You got yourself into debt; it's your responsibility. Now, it's time for you to get yourself out.

There are potential big tax implications as well. I am not an accountant by any means, so if you need more advice on debt forgiveness, speak to your accountant.

From my experience, you want to stay as far away from these "opportunities" as you can. I learned the hard way.

Being debt-free is an amazing accomplishment. Only one in five live with no debt, depending on what source you look at. When you have no debt, you can start to enjoy your money more – and that's why we are all here.

In my opinion, it is the largest and probably the most important step in achieving financial freedom. The reason why? You don't have to pay other people anymore!

You can now start paying yourself.

Once you've accomplished a debt-free lifestyle, you can really start to build your buffer and prepare your family for the future.

Good luck on this step in the journey. I believe in you.

STEP EIGHT

BUILD YOUR BUFFER

Congratulations! You are now debt-free.

Give yourself a pat on the back, take the wife out for dinner, or do something crazy just because you have earned it. After that, you can get back on track.

There is still a lot of work to be done. But the good news is that it's smoother sailing from here on out. I want to be clear. I am not saying that everything will now be easy – but hopefully, you are now in a groove to the point where you really don't know any other way but to live below your means, be responsible with your money, and ultimately account for every dollar that comes in and goes out.

Depending on what **debt** -crushing method you chose, somewhere along the line, you most likely have now become net positive (you have more money than what you owe).

Now it's time to build your buffer because financial freedom – although being much closer now – can still be a few years out. For us, if nothing changes, we will be millionaires before we turn 50, but I can see that timetable starting to accelerate already.

Remember, this is not a book about getting rich quickly. This is a lifestyle-changing book that will allow you to enjoy your money for the rest of your life. Financial freedom means different things to different people.

This is a template to help you achieve your own success. I hope that you end up doing better than we have!

Regardless, even if you only have a few thousand in your bank account – you still owe nothing, so you're worth something (financially speaking).

Did you know at my age (34), the median net worth is $34,000? Seems like a lot, doesn't it?

You can't retire on that.

With that said, the median net worth of a 65-year-old, which is when you should be retired or thinking about retiring, is only $189,000.

It's sad to think about an entire lifetime of work and nothing to show for it. Don't let that be you. You have already come this far.

Building your buffer could mean a lot of things – but for the sake of this chapter, we are going to go back to step six (start saving) and build upon what we already have.

The general rule of thumb is you want to have three to six months of your monthly expenses tucked away in case some sort of life-changing event occurs where you now were unable to work.

If you were suddenly out of work – bringing in no income - how long would you be able to survive in your current lifestyle before it all ran out?

A couple of months?

Less?

Yah, let's get that buffer nice and big.

If you haven't figured it out already – we lean more on the conservative side when it comes to money. So when I say three to six months, what I really mean is six months.

Go back to your budget.

The example we used in step five came to a budget of $3,640/month. Six months of that equals $21,840.

This is the amount you want to now save up AND NOT TOUCH.

It will be your new zero.

This is important to remember when we get to reconciling in the next chapter.

If you want to go with three months – power to you. But let me point something out.

A little thing called COVID-19 happened, and people were out of work for at least three months before businesses started to open back up; if they even had a job to go back to. Three months can go by real fast. So again, I like six. I feel like I am more secure.

My definition of financial security is *to be able to live the same way I do now for the rest of my life without having to bring in money*. If I want to retire at 50, I better have 30+ years of my expenses saved up to be able to do so. If I do – then I'm secure.

During COVID-19, nothing changed in our lives other than staying at home a lot more than I was used to. But financially, we were all set – which is a good feeling to have.

If you remember my 80/10/10 rule, by the time we were out of debt, we had also already built up a six-month buffer – so there is a good chance that you will be able to check both the debt box and the buffer box at the same time. If not, that is okay.

You Should Have More than One Account

It's time to start organizing your bank accounts.

We actually have two checking accounts, a savings account, a credit union account, two retirement accounts, one investment account, and a couple of other small things – but that is because I'm insane.

It's at four different banks, too.

The reason for these things is each account has a specific purpose, and that makes things easier for us.

You don't have to be as neurotic as I am – but I think it would be prudent for you to have at the very least three separate accounts. Before you freak out, HEAR ME OUT.

You can get away with two. Most people have a checking and savings account anyway. Be open to the idea of three. They will have the following tasks:

1. Checking #1 – Primary Operating Account – this account will be where most, if not all, of the action will take place. All your bills and expense categories will come in and out of here. Your paychecks will go into this account.
   Build this account to your six-month buffer. That will be your new $0. In other words, at the beginning of each month, you should start with this number ($21,840 in the example).
2. Savings – Keep your "emergency" savings from step five in this account. If you chose to save $1,000 – get it to one month's expenses. If you chose one month's expenses already ($3,640 in the example), you're already done. That will be your zero. You will only fall below that number in an emergency. But don't worry – we will be growing this account down the road, too.
3. Checking #2 – I recommend having this account at a separate bank which a specific purpose, like a major financial goal that you have. Currently, this account is for a down payment on our first home – so

I only put money into this account. I will not take it out until we are ready to tap into it for the house only. SIDE NOTE: I also have a second job that does not go into the operating account. 100% of that income goes into this account, untouched. Just a thought.

If you're married and have two incomes, there is a chance that one of you will make enough to cover all your expenses. You can get creative and use your other income to feed into a separate account.

See how fast that bad boy grows if 100% of one of your incomes goes somewhere untouched.

But the chapter is on buffers, so let's get back to it.

Remember all that money that you just put towards your debt? You don't have to do that anymore. Let your primary checking account grow to a six-month buffer. It won't take too long. If you want a shortcut, get a temporary part-time job. It will accelerate this process.

I enjoyed waiting tables for six months.

DO NOT START MOVING A TON OF MONEY AROUND UNTIL YOU HAVE YOUR BUFFER. You may have already been in the habit of putting 10% into your savings account each month – you can keep doing that if you want to – even if you already have one month saved in that account. You will have this step completed when you have done the following:

1. Six months of expenses are saved in your primary checking account
2. One month of expenses are saved in your savings account
3. You have opened an additional account (preferably at a different bank) and put in a minimal (nominal) deposit to get it started.

That's about it for this one. You can get creative. Find new ways to bring in income, or just wait for it to happen naturally through the good habits you have formed to this point.

You have now completed the infrastructure for long-term success. If at any point something happens in your life where you need to go back and re-start a step, you can do so.

Remember, start with getting your budget in order. Start saving. Crush your debt. Finish it all off by building your buffer.

Fall below your savings "zero"?
Build that backup, and then continue with the buffer.

Had to take on new debt? Pay that off quickly – then
re-build your buffer.

The process will never change.

I am so proud of you for making it this far. We've gone through the meat and potatoes. Time to put the cherries on top.

Not on the potatoes.

Let's build that wealth, dive deeper into reconciliation, talk briefly about investing, and touch on projecting future success, retirement, growing your assets, and more.

Are you enjoying your money yet? Well, you should be by now. The last steps will help you plan for continued enjoyment and (oh my god) maybe even financial freedom.

We can put a number on it.

And a date…

Let's continue.

STEP NINE

RECONCILING – HAMMER OUT YOUR GOALS

Have you ever opened your mobile banking just because you like to see how much money you have in your bank account? Well, maybe not yet.

By the time you have made it to this step, you will.

It feels good to be in a position where you don't have to worry about how the next month's rent will be paid – or having your entire world spin into a frenzy when you find out your "car inspection" will cost you $1,500.

You now have not only a good amount of cash on hand but also a little bit of financial security.

You won't lose your shirt if something goes wrong; you can live off what you have for several months if you have to. Better yet – once you reach this point, you will have created some incredible, life-changing, long-term habits that will benefit your life.

You can start having some more fun with your money, too. Reconciliation is one of my favorite things to do. I personally do weekly reconciliations because we have ONE credit card, and I pay it off every Friday as part of my reconciling. If you are in debt – remember - credit cards are the enemy.

Since we now never carry a balance, it works for us to gain certain travel points – but that's about it. We essentially use it for gas and dining.

If doing this step weekly is too much for you, I would recommend doing it twice per month at a minimum. It helps break up the work and keeps you tighter to your budget.

You would not want to end up in a situation where, at the end of the month, you realize you went way over budget in one of your sub-categories, only to have been prevented if you were a little more cognizant of what was left earlier in the month.

Fridays work best for me. I simply send a text to my wife with how much we have left in our spending categories.

You know one of the top reasons people get divorced is because of financial reasons?

I can honestly say Ashley and I have never gotten into a fight about money because we talk about it.

There are two types of reconciling we will focus on – weekly and monthly. Your weekly reconciliations are very simple. You are essentially tracking/writing down what you have spent in the last week.

Monthly reconciliation is when you round out the entire month, get back to "zero", and move money around based on what goal you are trying to achieve.

Sounds complicated, but it is very simple.

A couple of things to remember:

- Your operating account (probably main checking) is the one you use to deposit your income and withdraw for your expenses
- Your "zero" is your buffer. If you chose to save up three months of expenses, that number is considered $0 in your operating account. If you have six months saved up, it's the same thing. In other words, with a monthly budget of $4,000 – six months saved up is $24,000. You will start each month from here on out at $24,000. If you ever end a month below that amount, save back up, and then you can go back to moving money around.
- It's good to have a separate account(s) to make it less likely that you'll tap into your other monies.

When you reconcile weekly, you are essentially following these five steps:

1. Write down everything you have spent in the past week – I have a receipt tracking worksheet. Reach out if you'd like to see what ours looks like. Make sure you write it all down, big or small, and put them in the correct categories.
2. Add up your cumulative spending to date for this month. The key word is cumulative. So if you spent $1,800 in the first week of the month and then $1,200 in the second week of the month, your report should show that you've spent $3,000 so far this month. With a budget of $4,000, you will know that you can't spend more than $1,000 for the rest of the month.
3. Include any income you have deposited into your account. Subtract your monthly monies spent from your monthly income earned. Say you earn $1,000 per week. By the end of week two, you will have

$3,000 out but $2,000 in, for a net of -$1,000 (looks like ($1000) in excel).

4. Write down how much is in your bank account today. Subtract your "zero" from this number.
5. Compare your two numbers. They should (usually) match.

In a sense, you are looking at only two numbers – the one on your receipt worksheet (negative or positive number) and the number on your reconciliation worksheet (negative of positive number). If those two numbers match, then you know you did your job. Here is a visual.

Reconciliation Report:

	Starting Date	**Today's Date**	
	May 1st	**May 14th**	
Checking Acct	$24,000	**$23,000**	*($1,000)*

Receipt Tracker:

May 14th

Mortgage:	$1,500			
Car Payment:	$300	$400		= $700
Heat:	$100			
Groceries:	$85	$115		= $200
Dining:	$65	$85		= $150
Gas:	$30	$30	$40	=$100
Unforeseen:	$25	$150	$75	= $250

TOTAL SPENT: $3,000

INCOME THIS MONTH: $1,000 $1,000   = $2,000

NET FOR MAY = $2,000 – $3,000 = *-$1,000*

If you are off, go back through and see if you missed anything. I know I mentioned this advice before, but using mobile banking and debit cards make this process a hell of a lot easier.

If you take out cash , you can either set a sub-category for yourself labelled "cash" – sort of like having an allowance for yourself each month – or you can keep all your receipts and track it from there.

If you are a little bit off (maybe a $3.00-$5.00 lag in either direction), don't stress about it too much. This is not accounting where it has to be perfect unless you want it to be. At the end of the month, when you move money around, you will end up back at your "zero" anyway. Once you get in the habit of tracking everything, you will not be very far off.

SIDE NOTE: Even if you receive a $50 check from Grandma for your birthday, put that in the receipt worksheet because it increases the amount in your account, so you want to track it.

You won't claim it as part of your monthly take-home income, but it does count as a credit. Same for those few pennies of interest the bank throws your way each month. If it's on your statement, credit or debit, include it. It will make it more accurate.

So you have now reached the end of the month. We will start to move money between accounts based on what goal you are trying to achieve – or simply based on how you want to move your money around. At the end of the month, you will follow the first five steps listed above, but then you will add these three steps:

6.
    a. If the amount of money in your account is lower than what you started the month with, do nothing. You need to save back up to your zero. In other words, if on May 31st, you have $23,650 in your account – it's below your zero of $24,000. You must go back a step and replenish your buffer. This has not happened a single month since Ashley and I started, but it needs to be stated – so needless to say, this will be rare if you budgeted correctly.
    b. If the amount of money in your account is higher than what you started the month with – move that money around. I will give you an example from our current life. We are currently

saving up for a home. I would like to pay cash – but will not do anything less than 20% down on a home, so we are building that fund in a separate money market account. However, we still always make an additional contribution to our savings, as well as my investment account each month. Currently, 70% of what we net each month goes to home, 15% to savings, and 15% to long-term investment portfolio. You can determine for yourself where you want to put that extra money and what percentages to which purpose. Give every dollar a purpose.

7. Transfer the money based on your percentages to the appropriate accounts. Following our example, let's say we netted $1,000 at the end of May instead of a loss. That would mean we have $25,000 on May 31st in the account. I would take 70% ($700) and transfer that to our home account, 15% ($150) would be transferred from our checking to savings, and the last 15% ($150) would get transferred into our portfolio.

If this was the first month you did this, it would look something like this:

ACCOUNT	BEGINNING BAL	TODAY'S BAL
CHECKING	$24,000	$24,000
SAVINGS	$4,000	$4,150
HOME	$0	$700
PORTFOLIO	$0	$150
TOTAL	$28,000	$29,000

POP QUIZ. Did you notice something different in the numbers above that was not mentioned in this chapter?

What about these numbers seems off?

Did you answer the savings account? Then you would be correct. Remember, you built your buffer.

In this scenario, I am including the fact that you had already built a six-month buffer in your operating account and a one-month buffer in your savings for emergencies.

Also, notice that your checking account balance is the same at the beginning and end of the month. That's a good thing. No need to have tons of money sitting in a low-interest account when you can use it to build wealth or achieve other financial goals.

This is a simple example. I believe, in total, we have money going in and out of eight different accounts which I track.

Did I mention I was a little crazy?

Well, this could become you, too. It's a good crazy. There is no wrong way to do it because there is only one concept here that we all follow, regardless of how much you have.

8. Set up your next month. Open a new tab in excel, label it for the new month, and fill in your starting numbers. It would look like this:

ACCOUNT	BEGINNING BAL	TODAY'S BAL
CHECKING	$24,000	$24,000
SAVINGS	$4,150	$4,150
HOME	$700	$700
PORTFOLIO	$150	$150
TOTAL	$29,000	$29,000

Then, as you reconcile each week through the month, the column under "beginning balance" is already established, and "today's balance" will change as you type that in on any day that you choose to check back in and insert all your numbers on the receipt worksheet.

Sometimes I like to spend two minutes just typing in my checking balance on a day we get paid, even if it isn't a Friday – just because I like seeing the higher number. You will make this your own – but if you ever need help, you can reach out to me, and I can help you.

We will not go into too much detail here as I want you to get the basics down, but I will mention that it is good to set up a quarterly and an annual form of reconciling. It helps with long-term tracking, which is one of the last steps.

This is not something that you HAVE to do, but since you are setting a new budget for yourself at the end of each year, it's good to, at the very least, close out the previous year in a similar fashion.

That is essentially the nuts and bolts of reconciliation. You can always change how you move money around from month to month, depending on what you want to do.

As previously stated, when we were paying off debt, we would move 80% of our monthly net towards debt, 10% into savings, and 10% into investing, hence where the 80/10/10 rule came from. We moved to 70/15/15 when our new goal was a home.

Perhaps you have children, and you want to start tucking some money away for college. You could open a 529 plan or an HYSA and put a percentage into that. Hell, you could put 100% of what you net into something – a future new car, for example.

The last piece of advice I would give here is to have reconciliation be for some of your larger goals, building your future, increasing wealth, or towards some sort of retirement.

We will talk a little about investing and building for your future in the next couple of chapters.

Looking for any of the worksheets discussed in this chapter? Send us an email at njoyyourmoney@gmail.com.

STEP TEN

INVEST

As I stated at the beginning of this book – I am not a financial advisor, licensed CPA, or wealth management expert. I simply have found a method that has worked for my wife and me - and friends who have taken advantage of it. We wanted to share it with others, too.

This is an important step.

Planning for the future is of the utmost importance. The most common feedback I get from people who are independently wealthy is that they wish they had started sooner.

The earlier you start putting your money away to start working for you, the **sooner you'll see dividends increase exponentially** – even if it is just a few years sooner. At this point in the process, you have more than enough money to work with, so let your money start growing to allow you to be secure later in life.

Did you know that almost 2 out of 3 people in the United States have less than $10,000 in their retirement savings accounts? 45% have nothing.

What a sad thought – to have worked your entire life, and in the "golden years" when you are supposed to kick back and enjoy the remaining years of your wonderful life – you are exactly where you started.

Investing is a critical step to prevent you from becoming a statistic. If there is any piece of advice I can give, start today.

Not tomorrow.

Today.

Wait! Ryan, don't I have to complete all these other steps first before I can start investing? The simple answer is yes, but it is also no. You still need to complete all the previous steps before you start looking to invest with greater magnitude.

In that same breath, there are ways to start investing now without compromising the step that you are on.

I will share three options with you:

Company Match – A lot of employers set up a retirement account for you that you can contribute to. The most recognizable account is a 401(k) – but there are others out there, depending on what industry you are in.

THIS IS VERY IMPORTANT.

If your company offers a match to contributions you make on an annual basis, YOU NEED TO TAKE ADVANTAGE OF THIS.

I worked for a company that matched 100% of the first 5% and 50% of the next 3%. Simply put, what that means is if I made $1,000 in a week if I choose to put in a contribution of 5% ($50) – the company will also contribute $50. If I contributed 8%, they would contribute $65 ($1,000 x .05 = $50 + ($1,000 x .03) x .50 = $15 = $65). This is a no-brainer, folks. It's free money. Before inflation, over the course of a year (52 weeks), that would be $2,600 that you'd get FOR FREE.

To give you a better idea, using the same example above - if you were 30 years old and contributed $2,600 a year for the next 10 years – with an annual rate of return (from the market) of a modest 6% per year, by the time you turn 40 you will have over $35,000 dollars.

With a company match, that same account would have over $70,000. Want to retire by 65? With the company match, you will have close to $600,000 by that time.

One thing I want to point out is by contributing to your company match program, the money comes out of your paycheck.

Your take-home money will be less.

If this is going to make it really tight for you, you have a decision to make. Say it is $50. Can you find $50 to cut out of your budget and still stay net-positive each month? If you absolutely cannot, wait. If you think you can take advantage of this now, regardless of where you are in the process.

Talk to someone in HR and ask them how you can set this up.

Start with what your company is willing to match. Again, you are getting free money. That's like your boss giving you a $50 bill at the end of each week just as a thank you.

Again, this is only if you are still completing steps one thru eight.

NOTE: If your company does not offer a match, but they do have a 401(k) or similar program, it is still a good idea to start making contributions if you can swing it now. Your money grows in these accounts way faster than a savings account ever will, so my recommendation would be to figure out how much you could contribute out of each paycheck to at least get the ball rolling and create those investing habits.

We started with only taking $25 out of my wife's paycheck at the beginning. It didn't grow fast, but it was a starting place. You are able to set dollar amounts or percentages. Both options will be available to you.

Open an IRA – Let's be real. There are also a lot of employers that DON'T give you the employee benefit of having a retirement account. In fact, I would venture a guess that most don't. If you are not fortunate to have that option, you can always open an IRA (individual retirement account).

Here is where I would sit down with someone at your local financial institution to explore what would be the best option for you.

Investment Apps – There are so many apps out there, and some are much better than others. If you read reviews, you will always see a bunch of good reviews, as well as several negative ones. Many apps use the concept of "micro-investing," where they connect the account to your debit card and "round-up" your purchases, and those go into your investment portfolio that you get to choose from.

The issue with this is if you bought something for $10.99, it would round up the $.01 and invest that. It does not grow very fast. With that said, if you treat it like a long-term investment portfolio and make conscious contributions, you can get some good returns. If you aren't going to utilize the app long-term with significant contributions, it might not be worth it – but for many, it could be a good starting point.

Now I will tell you what I do. Remember, we have no debt, and we have our buffer built, so my recommendations are based on being on steps 9-12 for quite some time because they all pretty much work together.

Ashley and I have three accounts that we use for investing/retirement.

She has a 403(b) with her employer.

I have a 401(k) with mine.

I also set up an investment portfolio using one of the investment apps.

The number we use?

15%.

The reason?

When we got into steps 11 (projecting your future) and 12 (retirement), that amount at **our** current place in life will get **us** to where **we** want to be by the time **we** turn 50.

We won't – but I want to be in a place where, if we wanted to, we could retire by then. If you are already in your 50s, you might need to make significantly larger contributions to be able to get to a comfortable place by "normal" retirement age. Again, this is why it would be good to sit down with someone and get the advice that you need.

If you are in your twenties and you can start putting away 15% - you will be well off. The early thirties, you will still probably be okay. Again, each family has different circumstances, and you will be able to make projections on what will be best for your family.

We use 15%. It's a good number to use, and there are a lot of resources out there that use this number as a recommendation, so it has worked for us. Because of that, I also recommend it.

So, 15% of my paycheck goes into my 401(k) with my company match. Ashley's employer does not have a match, but we still contribute 15%.

Finally, at the end of each month, during reconciliation, I make an additional 15% contribution of what we net into my app. This book is not meant to promote one app over another, so I will not share which app we use. Nonetheless, we are on track to be able to retire when I am 53 and she is 51 – and I am okay with that.

Could we go to 20%? We could. Our current financial goal is to buy a house, so because we are focusing on that, most of our money is going towards a home.

On that note, I don't speak much about homes, but if you can purchase a house outright, that is the goal. If you have to finance nothing less than 20% down on a 15-year fixed loan, you will be ready to pay off early because that will become the only new debt that you possess. You are ready to buy a house once you:

- Are debt free
- Have a minimum of a six-month buffer
- Have a 20% down payment (if you can't pay in full)

But this chapter is on investing, so we will get back to that. I hope this will, at the very least, get you into the mindset that you must make a decision to invest.

There are plenty of books out there that focus specifically on investing, and you might become obsessed with making investments. This is not that book. But it needs to be a part of your journey to financial freedom. If you really want to enjoy your money, it's one of the best ways is to have your money start working for you.

That is what investing does in the simplest terms.

To close out this step, if you take nothing else from these pages, remember these things:

- The sooner you start investing, the better
- There is no one way to invest
- If your company offers a match, take advantage of it (FREE MONEY)
- Start where you are comfortable, but get to 15% (or more) as soon as you can
- The market will ebb and flow. Set a goal, don't freak out, stay the course.

And you've done it! You are on the path to a beautiful future. When I first started writing this book, I thought it would be ten steps. Something just didn't feel quite right because I often found myself asking, "Now what?" I also find it powerful to be able to check in with yourself to make sure that you are on the right track for the rest of your life.

It's one thing to be able to say you are **debt** -free with piles of cash and possess a strong level of comfort in the moment. It's another to be able to actually *know* where you want to be, *know* how long it will take you to get there, and *how much* it will take to get to *your* definition of freedom.

Even the great Dave Ramsey leaves you hanging with his 7th baby step – build wealth and give. Don't get me wrong. I have nothing bad to say about his program. It's incredible and has helped tens of thousands.

But if you are anything like me, being told that because now you have some money, you can now go out and enjoy it, share it, and grow it – good luck! It isn't enough.

Projecting your future and having a retirement timeline set, to me, closes that door. I don't want any unknowns because well – life happens. I want to know exactly where I will be and when – and so should you.

This is why we will conclude with the last two steps, starting with projecting your future.

I will give you specific financial thresholds that you will want to hit over the course of your life and by when to allow you to make those consistent self-checks. I mean, who doesn't want the comfort of knowing you will have long-term success?

I truly believe that this is a lifelong practice that will set up your children and even grandchildren for success, too. This is not set it and forget it. Well, done.

This is a lifestyle.

STEP ELEVEN

LONG-TERM SUCCESS – PROJECT YOUR FUTURE

After doing all this hard work, it is important to continue to hold yourself accountable to make sure that you are on track to meet your long-term financial goals.

We keep it very simple, if you can believe it, for this part. I do not recommend including assets such as homes, cars (which are depreciable assets), jewelry, etc. I would solely focus on the cash you are able to access – if you had to.

You can start your projections after a couple of months if you want to. I label this section "LIFETIME" in my workbook. In other words, over the lifetime of our money enjoyment plan, how much has our net worth (in cash) increased month to month?

I will give you an example of what I am talking about:

Say you made the agreement to start budgeting in March. You listed all your checking, savings, investment, retirement, HSA, and other – accounts – and wrote down how much is in each of those accounts.

This will give you your starting point. Using our story as an example, we started with a shade under $25,000 cash. Assume no debt.

Let's say by June, we will have $31,000. In three months' time, our net worth (in cash) went up $6,000 ($31,000 - $25,000 = $6,000). That is an average of $2,000 per month ($6,000 / 3 months = $2,000/month).

For us, we set goals strictly on dollar amounts of $100k, $250k, $500k, $1M, and *financial freedom*, which we use as having 25 years of income. More on that later.

So, let's take the first goal of getting to $100k. If we now have $31,000 – that means we have to earn another $69,000. At the current rate of $2,000/mo., it would take 34.5 months ($69,000 / $2,000 = 34.5), or just under three years to get to our first goal.

Don't let that frustrate you. I understand that three years can be a long time! Folks, I have never said this is a get-rich-quick book. What this does give you is a timeline.

Three years isn't fast enough for you? Pick up another job, get a side hustle, or you can start earning some passive income. Ask for a raise, trim down your budget, or get out of those high monthly car payments.

The good news is with each adjustment, you will also see your projections adjust. Most of the time, it's for the better. Sometimes it is worse. But you have a pathway.

Keep in mind you can always re-start your projections.

We are now 4.5 years into our plan. On average, our net worth has gone up close to $4,000 each month. By the end of our fifth year, Ashley will have completed her master's degree and will get a significant pay raise upon becoming a nurse practitioner. When we start the sixth year, there is a chance that we will be banking somewhere in the line of $6-8K a month, maybe more – I don't know.

What we can do is restart our projections with the money we have at the end of year five, our new starting place. Assuming a significant adjustment in our potential net worth increase month to month – it could speed up our projections with the new numbers.

In other words, we will have five years of data, which is great – but the new data is more specific to our long-term future.

QUICK TANGENT:

You can set as many goals and lay out as many projections as you wish. You want to pay for your son or daughter's college – you can project how long it will take you to get there. Want to get one account to a certain amount to put a down payment on a home? You can separate that account out of the mix and project that, too.

On that subject, many people ask me why I don't include homes in all of this. There are a few reasons:

- Not everyone has the goal of owning a home
- While you can sell a home for money, often one of three things happen:
    - People downsize – which is more cash in your pocket – which is what we are looking at

- o People go back to renting later in life – they sell their home (cash) and have a substantial amount of money they can use to apply to rent.
  - o Homes go into a trust, will, or are handed down – often, the children sell it for cash.
- While you do build equity in the home, I would rather keep that equity instead of tap into it for emergencies.

There are more, but I think that makes the point.

I don't want to overlook the most important part, which is *financial freedom* – that's the whole point of this book!

You may have a different idea of what financial freedom means than I do, which is okay. You can use the tools provided in this book to adjust to your wants and needs. I will remind you of what my definition of financial freedom is:

Financial security (freedom) is **to be able to live the same way I do now for the rest of my life without having to bring in money.**

To put it another way, if I were to spend the same amount of money I do now each year until the day that I die, without bringing in a single penny to make that happen, I am now free.

Here's how I figured that out. I want to retire at the age of 55. The average life expectancy in the United States in 2020 is about 78 years. I'm pretty healthy, so I used an expected age of death for me at 80 years. Because I have buffers for everything - let's say I luck out and live to the age of 85. Well, that means we will need to have 30 years stored away.

Let's break this down. If you follow a similar model, and your annual budget is $50,000, you will need $1.5M ($50,000 x 30 years) to feel comfortable knowing you will be able to make it. Yes, I understand $50,000 today will not be the same in 30 years. That is why having your money in investments is important because you will be able to stay ahead of inflation, in theory.

Want an additional buffer? Add 10-20% on top of that number. Whatever works for you.

I am currently projected to be clear for 30 years at the age of 62, and it continues to go down. It's not 55, I know that… but I can project that I will, if nothing else changes, be able to retire somewhere in that time. That's pretty exciting. Before the age of 60!? I'll take it.

I have a feeling it will be a lot sooner than that…

There you have it. I told you it was simple. Unlike any other goal-setting advice, you will hear all the time that it is important to set long-term goals. It's one thing to set those goals and hope they will come to fruition. It is another to know how long it will take to get there. It helps keep you focused. It also allows you to set smaller, short-term goals along the way.

I will say it one more time – don't let your projections deter you. In moments where you feel like you will not be able to accomplish anything, go back to your why.

We will not become millionaires until we are 53 and 49, respectively. That is almost 20 years from now! I don't let that bring me down; it drives me. I see it as a challenge. Change your mindset. Only 6% of people in the United States can say they are millionaires. Only 7% of those are under the age of 50. By my calculations, that is .0042, or .42% of the population, can say they are a millionaire before fifty.

If nothing else, my why – my wife, and my future children – deserve that. If we don't get there – it's not about the money. Funny thing to say in a book about money – but it's not.

If we don't hit that goal, we pivot, adjust, and keep on rolling. It's a hell of a lot better than week-to-week, paycheck-to-paycheck, or living in fear because you don't know what you'd do if your car broke down.

When you have the ability to project, you have the ability to mold your life the way you want it. Isn't that really what this is all about?

Have fun with it. Keep it realistic. Stay on track. I think Teddy Roosevelt said it best:

"Nothing in the world is worth having or worth doing unless it means effort, pain, difficulty…I have never in my life envied a human being who lived an easy life."

STEP TWELVE

ENJOY YOUR LIFE - RETIREMENT

I've been a college soccer coach for over a decade now. Working within the University, I am frequently perplexed by the mindset I observe from a number of students about the purpose of college, the process, and the plan.

Here are the answers I get to simple questions all the time:

Q: What is the *purpose* of college?

A: To get a degree so I can get a job and make a lot of money.

Q: So what's your *plan*?

A: Study hard and get good grades so I can graduate on time – to get a degree, job, and money.

This book is not on the pros and cons of college, whether it is beneficial, or what value it brings to our lives – we will save that for another conversation.

But look carefully… are you able to catch the issue with those statements?

It's a terrible plan.

Let's look at the process here:

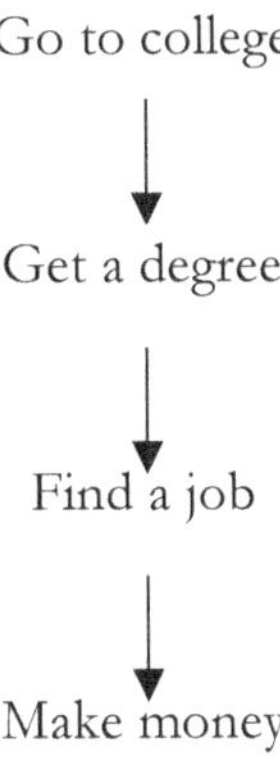

It's too linear. But this seems to be the mindset more often than not. I'll break it down another way.

The figure above pretty much says, "I am going to go to college to earn myself a degree. Once I have that degree, I am going to find myself a job that pays me a lot of money, and I am going to live a happy life."

WRONG! For most of us, this is a myth.

Here is the reality:

"Once I finish up college, I am going to have to find myself any job I can because the bill collectors are going to start calling in six months for me to pay my student loans back. If I am one of the lucky ones who is able to land a job in my field, if it's even a field that pays me well enough to cover my student loan payments AND start my life, any money I am making will be going back to them for the next twenty years, so to get ahead of the game, I am going to move back into my parents' basement and start saving."

Ryan, stop. This chapter is on retirement. What are you even talking about, and how does this relate to this chapter?

I'm glad you asked.

I'll get right to it. To be frank, this mentality and approach to college is almost the exact same approach that we take when it comes to retirement.

Q: What is the *purpose* of retirement?

A: To enjoy the rest of my life after a lifetime of work because financially, I'll finally be able to.

Q: So what's your *plan?*

A: Keep saving until I have enough where I feel like I can retire.

Look carefully…are you able to find the issues with THESE statements?

BINGO!

You said it; it's a terrible plan.

Here's the process that we as a society have created when it comes to our "golden years," the light at the end of the tunnel, the ever-coveted miracle of retirement:

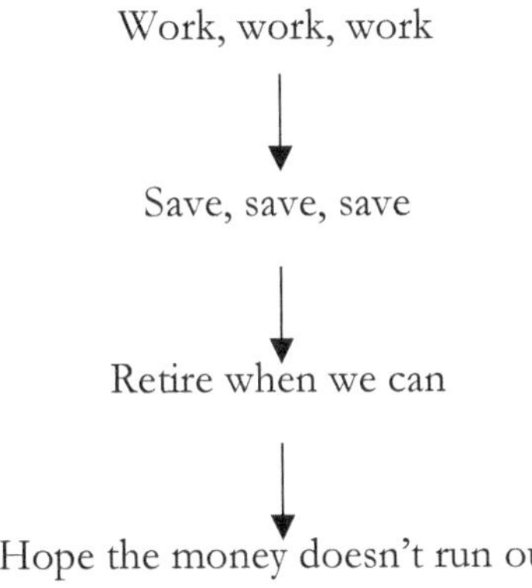

So you are pretty much saying, "I am going to dedicate, at a minimum, 40 years of my life to work. Meanwhile, I will start putting money away, little by little, so hopefully, once I get to my mid to late sixties, I won't have to work anymore, and I can focus on the things that I enjoy."

Here is the reality. I will provide you with ten facts that need to make you change your mindset NOW:

- Social security (if you'll even get it) will only account for about 40% of your income
- Over half of our retirees had to retire sooner than planned because of health reasons
- 3 out of 4 still plan on working after retirement – usually because they have to
- The average savings for families 56-61 is $163,000. How long can you live on that?
- However, the median retirement savings for ages 56-61 is $17,000
- Half of all Americans have $5,000 or less saved for retirement
- On average, for those who have a 401k, contributions average only 6%
- As of 2018, average social security is under $1,500/mo., or under $16,000 annually
- The average retired couple will pay $280,000 in medical expenses out-of-pocket
- 1 in five are completely reliant on Social Security

Soak all of that in.

You can go to any website and type in "retirement realities" or something along those lines and find dozens more startling bits of information like these.

Sadly, for most, retirement sounds something like this:

"We had a good plan, but life got in the way. We did what we had to do to survive. Now that I am unable to work, there are so many things I didn't realize. In the end, we just don't have the money. I hope my children and grandchildren will learn from our mistakes."

Folks, don't be a statistic. If you are reading this now with a pit in your stomach, you feel sick because there is no plan, no vision, and no hope – take today – not tomorrow, and put a plan in place.

I want to help you with that, too.

If you are behind, that is okay – just make sure to get all your debt paid off first and set up comfortable buffers for yourselves.

It might be necessary, come reconciliation time, to start throwing a lot of money towards your future until you get back on track. It might also be time to max out your contributions if you do have 401ks, etc.

I have mentioned several times in this book that if you are looking for specific advice around retirement (and well, everything else), talk to a professional. I am simply sharing with you a method that has worked for us, and I want to help you get there, too.

Doing my own research and seeing what fit in our lives is all we did, and I came up with a process (there's that word again) that will proactively keep us in check and let us know where we stand at any point in life.

As I write this chapter, I can safely tell you as of today, we will reach financial freedom before my 55th birthday – and our goal is to accelerate even that.

I can tell you I will not stop working in some capacity because I enjoy the things that I do.

But how nice is it to know?

I can also tell you that today, at this moment, we can live without ANY income for four years straight and not change a thing about our lives. Not bad after starting in debt at $85,000 and accomplishing this in less than five years.

Something must be working.

You can do it too.

Here are my three "pathways" to retirement – and yes, I look at all three.

1. The "Multiply by 25" Rule (also seen as "the 4% rule)

This is nothing new and innovative, and I didn't come up with it. But I added a little twist. Here is my definition of the "multiply by 25" rule:

What is our current annual budget? Multiply that by 25. That is how much we need.

For example, if your annual budget is $50,000, you will need $1,250,000. In other words, you will be able to live another 25 years on your current budget before you have nothing. Keep in mind that you might want to add another $250,000-$300,000 to cover medical expenses.

I am not saying that once you hit that number, you are now ready to retire. What I am saying is that once you've hit that number, you know that you can realistically live another 25 years *at your current budget* and be fine.

You might want to live more lavishly. You might bunker down and spend much less – I don't know you personally or what your goals are. This is just a checkpoint.

We are currently projected to reach this point when I turn 54 years old. I personally would not feel fully comfortable at that point to just pull the plug altogether, which is why I have two other methods.

2. The "What You Need Saved By" Rule

This, again, is something that you can look up, and it's a metric that I like to use. The "what you need to be saved by" rule simply tells you about how much you should have in savings by the time you hit certain ages.

I like this because it starts at the age of 30, and you can project out over the course of your life to see if you are on track.

For this, use your take-home income. We will use a take-home income of $100,000 for easy math. Here are your milestones:

By 30 years old	x1 income	$100,000 saved
By 40 years old	x3 income	$300,000 saved
By 50 years old	x6 income	$600,000 saved
By 60 years old	x8 income	$800,000 saved
By 67 years old	x10 income	$1million saved

I like this method because, again, it gives you some good milestones to hit. This would be something that you would have to decide on your own or with your spouse if you have one. If you are fortunate enough to have $1M saved, if you retired today, that's like saying that you have another ten years as if you were working, but you're not.

Having a $50,000 annual budget, you'd be "good" for another 20 years to get back down to zero minus the health cost buffer.

Right now, we are projected to hit the 67-year-old milestone at the age of 46 and 43, respectively. I'm not going to retire at 46 because we will run out of money too quickly. I might be more comfortable at the age of 67 to have the $1M PLUS medical expenses, as I think I'm going to die at 85…you might feel ready. This still doesn't fully capture everything. Let's look at the third method.

3. The "Years You Can (or want to) Retire" Rule

I know I can come up with a little bit of a better name for this, but this method, in a sense, combines the first two.

For this rule, we are looking at the annual budget (not take-home income) combined with the number of years you are able to sustain that budget if you don't work.

Finally, add in the number of years you will be able to live a retirement with that same budget. I'll break it down.

Again, I am assuming death at the age of 80. In my family, that would be pretty good, and I have a five-year buffer built in. For this process, I use 80 as the benchmark. So, if we wanted to retire at 60, that's 20 years of retirement.

Sticking with the $50,000 annual budget, here is how it would look:

Years of Retirement	Age at Retirement	Money Needed
10	70	$500,000
15	65	$750,000
20	60	$1,000,000
25	55	$1,250,000
30	50	$1,500,000
35	45	$1,750,000

You will see that this is essentially the "Rule of 25," but it is expanded to consider the opportunities to retire earlier. It also helps you see if you are on track to retire later if you can't set yourself up for a 25-year retirement.

Look at the supplemental material – it looks at what you currently have as a percentage of where you want to get.

So, if you were to retire today with $100,000 in your pocket, but you are 60 years old, you would only have 10% of the money you would probably need.

This is a different way to project because it looks at what you have, not what you are on pace to have.

For instance, I know that if I were 60 years old today, I would only have 17% of what we would need.

Good thing we have time and a plan in place.

In a different vein, everyone always asks what that "magic number" is. I don't think there is necessarily a "magic number" to retire on because we are all a little different.

For me, it's a combination of all the things we looked at:

First, we ask:

1.   How old are we now?

And finally:

2.   What is the lifestyle we want (annual budget) – how many years of that do we have?
3.   What is the money we want to bring in (annual take-home income) – how many years of that?
4.   How much of a medical buffer do we want to set, or will that come out of what we have?

So we all should be asking those questions to ourselves. You'll then come up with your own equation. When you do, shoot me an email. You have won.

I'll give you a possible example of an equation. If you're like me, you just want to know. Assume factors are wanting 10 years of income, 25 years of retirement, and $250,000 in medical expenses:

(# of retired years x annual budget) + (anticipated medical costs) = **magic number** + (what you want to make x # of years with net positive) = true number.

$$(25 \times \$50{,}000) + (\$250{,}000) = \mathbf{\$1{,}5000{,}000} + (\$50{,}000 \times 10)$$
$$= \$2{,}000{,}000$$

$$\$2{,}000{,}000 - \$1{,}500{,}000 = \$500{,}000 \text{ to leave to your children.}$$
If you like that number, retire.

So, $1.5M will get you there… but you will have zero after 25 years… and this doesn't consider the time value of money. The difference is the number of years you want to *pay yourself* and how much you will want to have left.

That brings your true number, and we are all a little different in deciding that.

That about does it for retirement. In the end, seek a professional if you are stuck or don't know what to do. If you take nothing else from this, do something now.

Today.

Not tomorrow.

Today.

Come up with a plan and start hoarding absurd amounts of money if you need to get you on track. If you only like one of these methods, go with that approach. If you find a combination that works best for you like we did, great.

The point is this is not a linear approach. Don't wait until you get close to retirement to start thinking about it.

Start today.

Oh, and you probably have figured it out, but if you are looking for any materials to help you track these types of things, I have a spreadsheet for that.

WHAT'S NEXT?!

You made it through. You no longer have to worry about where that next paycheck will come from, and you don't have to stress over whether you'll be able to keep the lights on next month. You've worked hard. It has taken a lot of time, effort, stress, sacrifices, and maybe even some tears.

BUT IT WAS WORTH IT.

You've done it. While you might not be completely where you want to be yet - because this is, in fact, a change in lifestyle for your lifetime – you at least have the confidence to know where you are going and how long it will take for you to get there.

Many people ask, "Where do we go from here"? The answer is simple:

PAY IT FORWARD.

There will be a point in your journey where you wake up one day and start thinking, "How can I help others?" You might even be at a gas station and be happy to buy those Girl Scout cookies (even though you don't like them) because you know it will help them out, and you can spare a few bucks.

It's a peculiar feeling the first couple of times when you don't find yourself making a game plan on why you won't be able to buy – or avoid eye contact with the man holding a bell at Wal-Mart.

There isn't an obvious moment – but it does happen.

That feeling when suddenly you want to help others as well.

Because you can.

One of my favorite quotes goes like this:

> "When you learn, teach. When you get, give."
>
> -   Maya Angelou

These words are simple yet powerful. You are now an expert on how to handle your expenses. Is there anything better than having the level of expertise you have acquired? And yet, there are millions of people out there who still struggle, who are lost, who need someone like you in their lives to show them the path.

AND YOU CAN DO IT.

In the time I have been writing this book – I haven't advertised at all. We've run into family, friends you have not seen in a while, or co-workers all the time.

Often, we get a question similar to, "How's life?" or, "What's new?"

My response: "It's been great!" Sometimes, people look at you sideways, so I go on to tell them about this book I am writing that will help people reach financial freedom; it will finally allow them to enjoy their money.

AND THEY ARE HOOKED.

I couldn't believe how many people close to me were looking for something (or someone) that could help them get their finances in order. In a few short months, I have already started consultations with close to a dozen families. There are plenty of people out there who help with wealth management, investing, day trading, real estate, or a number of other topics. What I have found is there are very few who help with our greatest needs: corralling our personal finances.

It's the most overlooked but most commonly taken-for-granted facet of our financial lives.

NOW YOU'RE ONE OF THOSE PEOPLE WHO CAN HELP.

I encourage it. If you want to, buy them this book and become the teacher yourself. A lot of this information (and there is A LOT of information) takes time to learn and grow. I can provide supplemental materials, video tutorials, and even the EYM community – but there was a process where you needed to learn, too.

Every family is a little different. It is a great feeling for someone to start fresh to know they have someone else in their corner to help.

We are in your corner, too. Use us. I feel it is important to be a constant resource to help people.

If you ever have any questions, please – there is no question too big or too small – send us an email. You can reach out to us directly at njoyyourmoney@gmail.com.

Another quote that resonates with me is this little nugget (I know I said not many quotes, but I can't help it):

"We make a living by what we get. We make a life by what we give."

- Winston Churchill

Giving is one of the most incredible, unforeseen lessons I have learned during our journey to financial freedom.

A big part of enjoying your money is simply being able to help others in time of need. Perhaps it's giving your parents a much-deserved weekend getaway just to say, "Thanks." Trust me, when you give, it feels 10 times better than when you receive.

It doesn't always have to be money, either. Go help someone rake leaves. Babysit for a family who needs a night out together. The number of possibilities is endless.

This is nothing that you must do – but I will tell you that no one dies saying they wished they made more money. You can have all the money in the world, and if you are fortunate enough to get into a position where you can help others AND DON'T – well, you've lived a fruitless, empty life.

We are blessed with the things we receive – and although you have put a lot of work into reaching your goals. It's now time to help others reach theirs.

Let me be clear. You are not a charity – unless that is your goal. Do not let people take advantage of you. You do have every right to say "No" to those who ask you for money. You are not obligated to give the homeless person on the street a dollar every time they ask.

You have worked hard to earn some net worth.

It does and can happen. There are people out there who are looking to bring you down. Even family and friends sometimes. How many stories have we all heard of an athlete making it to the professional level only to come with a large entourage of people who are trying to live off their success? This does happen.

You are not a doormat.

Don't let anyone make you believe that you "owe" them. With that said, you have earned the right to decide how you will enjoy your money. Giving is a great place to start.

I recently had a former player who started a new job reach out to me. We hadn't spoken in a few years, but she reached out because she wanted to start getting into delivering her "pitch" and start earning some income herself.

She didn't know anything about our position – simply that I was someone she looked up to who might be willing to lend an ear. I took it a step further. I asked her what it took for her to reach her next goal, and I helped her get there.

In the end, it was only $100 – but if you asked me five years ago whether I had $100 to spare to help someone else out, I couldn't. At this point in my life, we could – so I wanted to help. Moments like this will happen to you, too.

So, in the end – give, share, teach, learn, help, and grow. When we all give a little, we can accomplish some great things. At the same time, keep yourself in check.

I have mentioned so many times on these pages that we are all a little different. Do what makes you happy, but don't put yourself in a position that reverts you back to when things were difficult.

The good news is, if that happens, you know how to get back here again, too.

It's your money. Go enjoy it.

CONCLUSION

It's a bit strange, but it took me the longest time to write this final chapter. It had nothing to do with it coming to an end and certainly had nothing to do with me struggling with closure; we get shit done.

I believe this because, in the end, there isn't a whole lot more to say.

We have gone through all the steps:

1. Find Your "Why:
2. List Your Financial Goals
3. Project Your Income
4. Track Your Expenses
5. Set Your Budget
6. Start Saving
7. Crush Your Debt
8. Build Your Buffer
9. Hammer Out Your Goals
10. Invest
11. Project Your Future
12. **Enjoy Your Life***

Then, two things hit me square in the face.

Without intention, for the first time, I realized something:

Almost every single step in the process uses the word "your." In the end, this is your life…which led me to the second thing:

We have found a way to enjoy our lives – all I have ever wanted is to help others reach their full potential and enjoy theirs, too. It's the coach inside of me.

It wasn't until that very second that I realized where this ends is actually the beginning. This book is titled <u>Enjoy Your Money in 12 Easy Steps</u>, but it ends with "Enjoy your life".

This is not a book about money. This is not a book about financial freedom. The pages of this book are a pathway that we have lived - which show how to reach the point where you can live a happy life without the fear of money and the burdens it places on so many.

The cliché, "money doesn't buy happiness," is one I believe. There are plenty of people with money who are not happy. Conversely, there are many who are fully happy and have nothing.

Why can't we have both?

This is not the end. This is simply the beginning.

This is the beginning of a journey (a word I use often) that will lead you to a point in your life where you will be able to say you have been able to accomplish something that so few are able to do.

This book was not about money, after all.

This book is about sharing. This book is about family. This book is about growing, communicating, and goal-setting. It's about relationships; it's about strength.

It's about passion. This book is about Joy.

We want to thank you for allowing us to share our story with you. Everything in this book is real (except for John and Sarah, sorry). It is a summation of the lessons we have learned from the beginning of our journey to now – and it's far from over.

There are so many things that Ashley and I still want to accomplish, and I look forward to hearing your stories of accomplishment as well. I see a community being built from this: a system of support.

If you cannot remember those six little words Ashley said to me on that plane heading towards Ireland for our honeymoon – I'd like to repeat them.

"Okay – but let's enjoy this first."

Don't let life get in the way. Your journey will be different than ours. You never get these moments back; they are gone forever.

Maybe in the end, this book is a love story because I found my why, and I've enjoyed every moment spent with her.

Find your why and hold onto it. You'll thank me in the end.

Enjoy Your Life!